VAGUS

NERVE

The Ultimate Guide to Learn How to Access the Healing
Power of the Vagus Nerve with Self-Help Exercises to
Overcome Anxiety, Depression, Inflammation, Chronic
Illness, PTSD and Trauma

NATHAN BLAIR

CONTENTS

INTRODUCTION

The vagus nerve, or pneumogastric nerve, is the tenth pair of cranial nerves of the total twelve, present in human beings, and the main representative of the nerve fibres that make up the parasympathetic nervous system.

The parasympathetic system is responsible for all involuntary bodily reactions that respond to situations of "rest", "energy recovery", contrasting and balancing the actions of the sympathetic system, which on the contrary, has a stimulating, exciting, and contracting function. (fight-or-flight reaction)

After a period of physical stress and alert, governed by the sympathetic system, a relaxation process must be established, governed instead by the parasympathetic system, which allows the recovery of the energy consumed and the performance of some vital functions of our body.

This is where the vagus nerve comes into play, which, by inhibiting prolonged flight or fight responses of the sympathetic system, restores the homeostatic balance of our body, which is fundamental for our good health.

The vagus nerve is an incredible part of our body. It is long, sinuous and powerful. It is unique and complex.

Inside the human body, it makes a long path: from its emergence in the medulla oblongata, it crosses the jugular hole, passes through the neck, descends into the thorax and, from there, reaches the abdomen.

In its course towards the abdomen, it establishes numerous connections: with the external auditory canal, the pharynx, the larynx, the oesophagus, the trachea and the bronchi, besides administering nervous fibres to the heart, the stomach, the pancreas and the liver.

This nerve is important for body functions such as digestion, breathing, heartbeat, eating, swallowing, speaking, clear sight and more.

Therefore, as it participates in the regulation of the functions of almost all internal organs, it is important that the vagus nerve functions properly otherwise your body would be in complete disarray.

Each of us have a certain degree of basal vagus nerve functioning, but it is possible to strengthen and modulate it through specific techniques and exercises.

By learning to stimulate and activate the powers of the vagus nerve, you will significantly improve your health and facilitate a natural pathway that the body can use to heal and repair itself naturally.

Vagus nerve stimulation will help you reduce chronic inflammation, overcome migraines, reduce symptoms of chronic auto-immune disease, depression, anxiety and more.

There are many books on this subject on the market, and thank you again for choosing this one! Every effort has been made to ensure that it is full of as much useful information as possible, and we hope you enjoy it!

THE VAGUS NERVE

WHAT IS THE VAGUS NERVE?

Simply put, the vagus nerve is the command center of your inner nerve center and regulates all the important organs. It is the longest cranial nerve, starting in the brain behind the ears and branching in several directions to connect to all the major organs in the body. It is also a fundamental element of the parasympathetic nervous system and affects breathing, digestive function, heart rate and mental health.

It is the 10th of the 12 cranial nerves that, according to the Encyclopedia Britannica, extend directly from the brain into the body as a complex root network.

Although we call it the singular vagus nerve, it is actually a pair of nerves that spring out from the two opposite sides (left and right) of the elongated spinal part of the brain stem.

These nerve networks act as communication channels between the brain and the many systems and organs in the body; whilst controlling the body's response during rest and relaxation. It is responsible for actions such as the transportation of sensory information from the skin of the ear, and the muscle control that you use to swallow and to talk.

The word "vagus" simply means "wanderer" because it travels all over the body, from the brain to the fertility organs, and everywhere else; distributing fibers in the external ear canal, pharynx, larynx, trachea, bronchi, lungs, large blood vessels, heart, esophagus, stomach, spleen, pancreas, stomach, intestines and glands. These produce enzymes and anti-stress hormones (such as acetylcholine, prolactin, vasopressin, oxytocin) which affect digestion, the metabolism and of course the relaxation reaction.

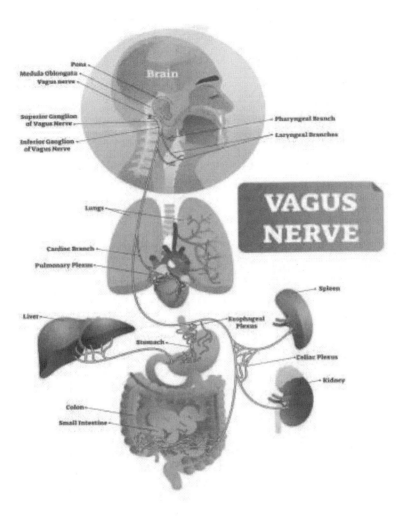

It is very easy to stimulate the vagus nerve, and therefore improve overall physical and emotional health. Your vagus nerve must be in order so that your body works well. Your organs depend on the vagal tract to regulate things like:

-       Hunger hormones and food intake
-       Inflammation
-       Anxiety and feelings of fight or flight
-       The immune response

WHY IS THE VAGUS NERVE SO IMPORTANT?

It is an important nerve for every organ with which it is in contact. As the vagus nerve travels through the body it helps control heart rate and blood pressure, and prevents heart disease. In the liver and pancreas, it controls the glycemic balance and prevents diabetes. When it goes through the gallbladder, the vagus nerve helps release bile, which helps your body flush out toxins and break down fat. In the bladder, this nerve promotes general kidney function, blood circulation and thus filtration in our body. When the vagus nerve reaches the spleen, activation reduces inflammation in all target organs. This nerve even has the ability to regulate fertility and orgasms in women, and it has a very important connection with the digestive system.

It is the vagus nerve that is in charge of the increase in gastric acid and the digestive secretion of the juices to facilitate digestion in the stomach. When stimulated, it can also help you absorb vitamin B12. If it doesn't work properly, you can expect serious bowel problems like colitis, IBS, and inflammation.

An inactive or blocked vagus nerve can destroy the soul and the body.

The vagus nerve also helps control anxiety and depression in the brain. The way we communicate is closely related to the vagus nerve, as it is linked to the nerves that connect our ears to speech, coordinate eye contact, and regulate expression. This nerve also has the ability to affect the release of hormones in the body, which make our physical and mental systems work well.

While some nerves have sensory or motor functions, the vagus nerve has both. Sensory and motor fibers branch from the heart, intestines, and lungs to other internal organs, including the gallbladder, spleen, liver, kidneys, and beyond.

The sensory duties of the vagus nerve are divided into two components:

Somatic Components - These are sensations on the skin or in the muscles

Visceral Components - These are sensations that are felt in the organs of the body

THE SENSORY FUNCTIONS of the vagus nerve include:

- Provide information about the somatic sensation of the skin behind the ear, the outer part of the ear, and some parts of the throat
- Providing visceral sensation information for the larynx, esophagus, lungs, trachea, heart, and most digestive tract
- Plays a small role in the taste sensation near the root of the tongue

THE MOTOR FUNCTIONS of the vagus nerve include:

- Stimulating the muscles of the throat, larynx and soft palate - the fleshy area near the back of the palate
- Stimulating the muscles of the heart to lower the resting heart rate
- Stimulating involuntary contractions in the digestive tract. This involves the esophagus, stomach, and most of the gut, which allows food to move through the airways.

The vagus nerve not only controls important motor and sensory functions, but is also the motor of the parasympathetic nervous system. **The Parasympathetic Nervous System** is a part of the autonomic nervous system along with the sympathetic nervous system.

The Autonomous Nervous System is responsible for managing a series of automatic, unconscious and involuntary activities related to the maintenance of homeostasis in the body, such as heartbeat, blood pressure or digestion.

The Autonomous Nervous System is divided into three subsystems:

- SYMPATHETIC - regulates the functions that require the use of stored energy, fight-or-flight reactions
- PARASYMPATHETIC - regulates "rest", "energy recovery" functions
- ENTERIC - regulates the complex of intestinal activities, through about 100 million neurons, and the secretion of more than thirty neurotransmitters.

The sympathetic and parasympathetic branches consist of a series of nerve pathways (axons) that reach the internal organs to stimulate or slow down, with their action, specific activities (e.g. increased muscle blood flow) but also in obtaining information.

The sympathetic nervous system works like an accelerator pedal in a car. It triggers the fight or flight reaction and supplies the body with an explosion of energy so that it can react to perceived dangers. The parasympathetic nervous system acts as a brake. It promotes the "rest and digestion" reaction, which calms the body as soon as the danger is over.

When the sympathetic nervous system triggers the flight or fight reaction, there are a variety of physical changes. Adrenaline begins to pump into the body. Heart rate and respiratory rate are accelerated, digestion slows down or stops, blood vessels contract, and muscles contract to fight or flee.

The parasympathetic nervous system is responsible for bringing the body back into homeostasis. After times of stress and anxiety, this "calm" state is caused by the release of a neurotransmitter called acetylcholine.

The harmonic activity of the two branches of the Autonomous Nervous System is reflected in a condition of general psychophysical well-being, a high level of energy, a state of remarkable vitality and, above all, the absence of the malaises typical of the prevailing action of one of the systems.

Nervous system

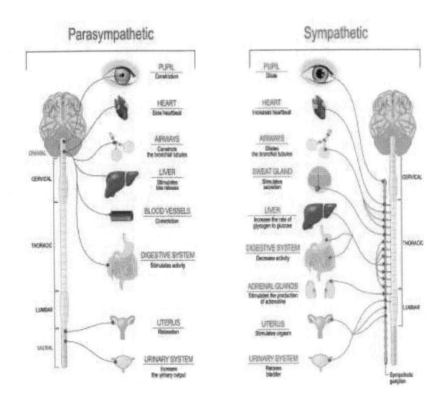

THE FUNCTIONS OF THE VAGUS NERVES

The vagus nerve is a key factor for optimal health, especially when it comes to getting into a parasympathetic or relaxed place. Below are some of the various ways the vagus nerve affects the body:

Connects The Brain to The Digestive System

Large parts of the vagus nerve extend to the digestive system. If you have ever felt anything from your intestine, it is up to your vagus nerve. The vagus nerve is what connects the brain to the intestine and sends information back and forth. This can also be called the 'gut-brain axis'. Your gut informs your brain of electrical impulses described as "action potentials". The nerve is known for stimulating digestion before someone eats anything. It sends signals to the gastrointestinal tract to start the production of gastric juices in preparation for digestion. If the vagus nerve is not at its best, digestion is not optimal.

According to the "Nerves and Nerve Injury Volume 1" manual, about 10% to 20% of the vagus nerve cells connected to the digestive system send commands from the brain to control the muscles that carry food through the intestine. (Academic Press, 2015). The movement of these muscles is then controlled by a separate nervous system that is integrated into the walls of the digestive system.

The rest of the 80% to 90% of the neurons transport sensory information from the stomach and intestines to the brain- the brain-gut axis. It alerts the brain to the state of muscle contraction, the speed of food intake through the intestine, and feelings of hunger or satiety. A study in 2017 found that the vagus nerve is so closely connected to the digestive system that nerve stimulation can improve Irritable Bowel Syndrome.

Several years back, many researchers found that this brain-gut axis has another influence - the bacteria that live in the gut. This microbiome speaks with the brain through the vagus nerve and not only affects food intake, but also mood and the inflammatory response. This emerges from a 2014 report published in 'Advances in Experimental Medicine and Biology'. Much of the existing research relates to experiments with mice and rats, rather than with humans. Still, the results are remarkable, showing that changes in the microbiome can cause changes in the brain.

The Vagus Nerve Helps Your Heart

Your heart can be considered one of nature's best-designed structures (you might even call it a work of art).

It consists of different tissues and is structured in such a way that it receives different electrical impulses that influence the way it beats.

The vagus nerve is in charge of controlling the heart rate via electrical impulses to specialized muscle tissue- the heart's natural pacemaker- in the right atrium, where the release of the neurotransmitter acetylcholine slows the pulse. An increase in heart rate requires inhibition of vagus nerve stimulation, which means that no acetylcholine is released. One of the parameters that determines the correct health of your heart muscle (your heart) is the measurement of so-called Heart Rate Variability, which measures the time between each of your heartbeats.

In addition to this, HRV is useful in assessing the health of your vagus nerve and its ability to positively influence your heart.

The higher your HRV, the better the health of your vagus nerve will be, and the greater your ability to recover from any strains and stressful events will be.

The Vagus Nerve Helps You Breathe in and

Out

Your vagus nerve sends signals to your lungs to perform the breathing actions which are composed of inhalation and exhalation cycles.

To do this, your vagus nerve uses the neurotransmitter acetylcholine.

Acetylcholine tells your lungs to breathe deeply and take in oxygen that replenishes your life energy. This is one of the reasons why botox- often used for cosmetic purposes- can be potentially dangerous as it disrupts your acetylcholine production.

The Vagus Nerve Helps You Relax

Many of us are unaware of the great hidden power that the vagus nerve has in helping us to relax.

When you find yourself in a condition that causes increased stress, your sympathetic system triggers the so-called flight or fight response: fight or run.

When this happens, stress hormones (cortisol and adrenaline) are released inside your body.

The vagus nerve counteracts this physical and nervous alteration by releasing acetylcholine and oxytocin in order to increase your sense of relaxation.

People who have suffered major trauma both physically and emotionally have a better chance of recovering if they have a stronger and healthier vagus nerve.

The Vagus Nerve Increases Memory Retention

A study by the University of Virginia has shown that stimulating the vagus nerve by encouraging the release of norepinephrine can help strengthen memories. This could have a huge impact on people with memory problems or people with Alzheimer's disease.

The Vagus Nerve Helps Reduce Cellular Inflammation

Stress, various traumas, illnesses, wounds, disorders of various kinds, excess or lack of activity and disorderly nutrition lead the body to the onset of cellular inflammation.

Some inflammation after an injury or illness is normal. However, chronic inflammation is involved in many modern diseases; including sepsis, cancer, heart disease and autoimmune rheumatoid arthritis. Since your vagus nerve is involved in the management of the various organs, it receives signals that indicate an increase in possible inflammatory processes.

When the vagus nerve detects inflammation (for example, through the presence of an anti-inflammatory cytokine or a substance called tumor necrosis factor), it communicates with your brain by causing it to release a variety of neurotransmitters and chemicals that help you turn off inflammation by activating your immune response.

The Vagus Nerve Promotes the Health of Your Liver

The Vagus Nerve regulates insulin secretion and helps you maintain glucose homeostasis within your liver.

Homeostasis is defined as the state of balance between internal physical condition and the release of chikic agents that your body puts in place to compensate for any imbalances.

The Vagus Nerve Promotes the Release of Bile

The vagus nerve is responsible for inducing your gallbladder to release bile, which is essential for the digestion of fat and the reduction of toxins in your body.

The Vagus Nerve Controls the Function of Your Kidneys and Bladder

The overall function of your kidneys is largely regulated by your vagus nerve, which increases blood flow and keeps glucose levels within physiological limits.

When your vagus nerve is properly activated, it releases dopamine into your kidneys, decreasing the pressure due to the sodium that is expelled from your kidneys.

Since the vagus nerve is connected to the bladder, this means that if the activation and stimulation of the vagus nerve is low, you will tend to urinate more.

The Vagus Nerve Is Involved in The Emission of Speech

Your vagus plays a part in the function of your larynx, the phonation organ that controls the sound and your vocal peak.

This nerve controls the way you breathe and protects you from choking on food by controlling your swallowing when you swallow part of your meal.

The Vagus Nerve Controls your Sense of Hunger

Numerous studies and field evidence show that obese and overweight people have a low vagal tone (the power of your vagus nerve).

This means that your vagus nerve, if you are in this condition, is not able to read the signs of satiety of your stomach.

Therefore, if you are in a condition of low vagal activation you will have to eat a lot more to reach your sense of satiety.

Your vagus nerve transmits signals to your brain in order to start your digestive process.

It also produces spontaneous contractions of your intestine that allow food to travel through the digestive tract.

The Vague Nerve Helps Releave You from Stress

Your vagus nerve releases acetylcholine, which removes

adrenaline and cortisol from your stress response and activates your body's natural relaxation response so you can relax, rest, and let go.

The problem is that our current culture encourages us to be so overly busy, so overly stimulated that we run in stress mode almost all of the time without knowing it. We are so used to stimulation that we don't know what real relaxation looks like, let alone how to do it.

Instead of practicing a natural rhythm between activity and rest, we are hyperactive. And we are so conditioned that we feel guilty if we don't always do something, or we get bored if we are not stimulated and entertained. As a result, anxiety, irritability and insomnia are constant companions. This prevents us from resting deeply and sets us on the path to chronic diseases such as cancer.

The Vague Nerve Improves Your Mood

Anxiety and depression are 'sensations' found all over the world. The World Health Organization has repeatedly affirmed that anxiety and depression are the most 'serious' emotional dysfunctions in the field of human health.

The bacteria inside your intestine are able to influence your emotions and activate the consequent responses of your vagus nerve.

Stress and depression can cause abdominal disorders, such as dysentery or stomach pain, and proper stimulation of the vagus nerve can help you change the way your body responds to certain situations that often cause unintended and uncontrollable emotional reactions.

VAGAL TONE

Vagal tone is an internal biological system that represents the activity of the vagus nerve.

The most widely used procedure for the quantification of vagal tone is the study of processes that are modified by the action of the vagus nerve, specifically heart rate and heart rate variability. In general, it can be said that an increase in vagal tone (and therefore a vagal activation) is associated with an increase in cardiac variability and a decrease in heart rate.

Heart rate is the rate of contractions or heartbeats measured by the number of beats per minute.

Heart Rate Variability (HRV)

It was once believed that the heartbeat at rest was monotonous and regular as with a metronome (60 beats per minute equals one beat per second).

Subsequently, research in the cardiology field revealed that the time that passes between one beat and the next is more or less variable.

This spontaneous change in the rate of the heart contraction was seen to be correlated with the influences exerted by the branches of the sympathetic and parasympathetic nervous system on the heart muscle and with the pressure interactions of respiratory activity.

In fact, the heart rate increases with inhalation (to speed up the flow of oxygenated blood) and decreases with exhalation, and Heart rate variability is the amount of heart rate fluctuation between inhalation (when it naturally accelerates) and exhalation (when it naturally slows down).

The difference between these two frequencies essentially measures the vagal tone. If your heart rate variability (HRV) is high, your vagal tone is also high.

A Higher vagal tone means that your body can relax faster after stress.

Studies which have been published showed a great feedback between high vagal tone, excellent physical health and improved emotional health.

A High Vagal Tone improves the functioning of many body systems, which leads to:
-   Better blood sugar regulation
-   Reduced risk of stroke and cardiovascular diseases
-   Lower blood pressure
-   Improved digestion through better production of basic and digestive stomach
-   Reduced enzymes and migraines.

A higher vagal tone is also associated with a better mood, less fear and more stress resistance.

Low Vagal Tone is associated with cardiovascular diseases and stroke, depression, diabetes, chronic fatigue syndrome, cognitive impairment and much higher rates of inflammatory diseases (rheumatoid arthritis, inflammatory bowel diseases, endometriosis, autoimmune diseases of the thyroid, lupus and more).

It is interesting that studies have even shown that the vagal tone is transmitted from mother to child. People who are depressed, anxious, and angry during pregnancy have less vagal activity. When the baby is born, the newborn also has low vagal activity and low levels of dopamine and serotonin.

Increase Your Vagal Tone

If your vagal tone is weak, don't worry - you can take steps to increase it by stimulating your vagus nerve.

While there are more invasive procedures aimed at stimulating the vagus nerve with electrical impulses, there are other less invasive techniques that can be used as part of a regular wellness program. This includes breathing exercises, meditation, massage, cold therapy, exercise, flow states and even personal social connectivity.

Refine your personal care with vagus nerve regulation strategies that you can use from the comfort of your own home.

VAGUS NERVE DYSFUNCTION

WHAT CAN DAMAGE THE VAGUS NERVE?

Several conditions, morbid or not, include among their various complications the damage of the vagus nerve.
Among these conditions, we should mention:

-Diabetes Mellitus Type 1 And Type 2

Diabetes mellitus is a metabolic disease, caused by a defect in secretion and/or action of insulin, a hormone essential for the passage of glucose from blood to cells. As a result of lack of secretion and/or malfunctioning insulin, blood glucose levels (blood glucose) rise, resulting in a condition known as hyperglycemia. In the long run, hyperglycemia leads to the deterioration of blood vessels that supply certain nerve structures, including nerves such as vagus, with oxygen and nutrients. Without oxygen and nutrients, any nerve, tissue or organ in the body undergoes a process of deterioration, more properly referred to as necrosis.

The whole process described above, culminating in the necrosis of certain nerves, is called diabetic neuropathy: "neuropathy" refers to the damage/bad functioning of nerves; while "diabetic" refers to the fact that neuropathy has diabetes as its trigger cause.

Diabetes mellitus is the most frequent cause of gastroparesis.

-Parkinson's Disease

This is a neurological disease of progressive character, which begins with the slow degeneration of the neurons of substantia nigra. The substantia nigra (or black substance of Sommering) is an area of the central nervous system, located between the midbrain and diencephalon, responsible for the production of dopamine. Dopamine is a fundamental transmitter for the harmonic and fast execution of movements.

In people affected by Parkinson's disease, the degeneration of substantia nigra cells coincides with the reduced presence of dopamine in the bloodstream. The reduced production of dopamine first leads to motor problems and then to other neurological problems, such as deterioration of the vagus nerve.

-Scleroderma

This is a chronic inflammatory disease of connective tissue, which mainly affects the skin, but can also extend to blood vessels, certain internal organs (heart, lungs, etc.) and the nervous system (nerves in particular).

-Anorexia Nervosa And Bulimia Nervosa

These are two eating disorders, resulting from a fear of gaining weight.

Self-induced vomiting, which is a typical reaction of people suffering from these disorders, increases the activity of the vagus nerve beyond the limit of tolerance and causes its deterioration.

-Amyloidosis

It is the medical term for a group of diseases characterized by the accumulation, often extracellularly, of the so-called amyloid fibrils. Insoluble, amyloid fibrils impair the function of various tissues and organs of the body, including nervous structures.

-Bariatric surgery or gastrectomy

Bariatric surgery is a therapeutic option for people with severe obesity, as it is a procedure that promotes weight loss.

Gastrectomy, on the other hand, is the surgical treatment of total or partial removal of the stomach, reserved for people with a tumor in this fundamental organ of the digestive system.

-Cervical Arthrosis

This is a very common pathology related to wear and tear of the joints between the cervical vertebrae. This often causes the vertebrae to move closer together and the nerves that pass through the intervertebral holes to compress.

-Atlas Misalignment

At the neck level, the vagus nerve has a diameter of 2-3 mm. It runs along the internal jugular vein and the carotid artery, just in front of the Atlas vertebra. Consequently, if the Atlas is not correctly aligned, the vagus nerve is the first to be affected, generating the classic symptoms of vagal compression.

Depending on the extent and type of movement of the Atlas in relation to its optimal position, pressure and thus inflammation of the vagus nerve and/or other cranial nerves may occur.

-Incorrect Posture

If you stand for a long time without changing position or if you sit with an incorrect posture of the cervical tract, you may experience inflammation of the vagus nerve due to the compression effect exerted by the muscles and cervical vertebrae.

-Persistent Stress and Anxiety

Severe stress or pathological anxiety can cause compression and inflammation of the vagus nerve. This is mostly related to the constant state of contraction which the muscles of the cervical tract are in when you are experiencing tension about something.

-High-fat Diet

Although the exact correlation has not yet been fully clarified, it seems that a high-fat diet may contribute to inflammation of the vagus nerve. The connection could be related to the fact that an excess of fat causes a state of general inflammation in the body.

SYMPTOMS OF VAGUS NERVE DYSFUNCTION

The vagus nerve is a long, twisted bundle of motor and sensory fibers that connects the brain to the heart, lungs and intestines. It also branches off to touch and interact with the liver, spleen, gallbladder, ureter, female fertility organs, neck, ears, tongue and kidneys. It stimulates our involuntary nerve center - the parasympathetic nervous system - and controls unconscious bodily functions over everything from keeping our heart rate constant to the digestion of food, breathing and sweating. It also helps control blood pressure and blood sugar balance, helps release bile and testosterone, promotes general kidney function, stimulates the secretion of saliva and helps taste control.

Without the vagus nerve, the key functions that keep us alive would not be maintained.

The vagus nerve is really critical to your overall health and is closely linked to various organs and systems in the body.

The vagus nerve has fibers that innervate practically all of our internal organs. The management and processing of emotions takes place via the vagus nerve between the heart, brain and intestine, which is why we have a strong intestinal reaction to intense mental and emotional states.

When the function of the vagus nerve is impaired, a whole series of symptoms can occur:

-Nausea and Digestive Problems

We have seen that the vagus nerve is an important nerve in

connection with digestive functions.

It is therefore logical to think that when it does not work well or when it is too active, digestion can be affected.

In particular we might experience nausea, stomach acidity, gastric or intestinal swelling.

-Problems of Tiredness or Non-Restful Sleep

One of the functions of the vagus nerve, as we have seen, is to activate itself in moments of relaxation, allowing us to recover properly.

Those who have a poorly functioning vagus nerve often have a poorly restful sleep, and therefore also experience tiredness during the day.

-Sprains, Fainting Sensations, Lowering of Blood Pressure

The vagus nerve, being an active nerve in moments of relaxation, tends to lower the pressure.

A sudden and excessive stimulation of the vagus nerve can lead to a sensation of fainting.

-Headaches and Migraines

The suboptimal function of the vagus nerve is associated with increased incidence of migraine and headaches.

This association is so strong that one of the most recent treatment systems for migraines and headache is a pacemaker that can electrically stimulate the vagus nerve.

-Thermoregulation Problems (Cold Hands and Feet)

The vagus nerve is a peripheral vasodilator: when stimulated and well-functioning, it increases blood flow to the extremities.

If the vagus nerve does not have good activity, the person affected can often have cold hands and feet.

It is no coincidence that when we are agitated (so the vagus nerve is completely non-functional) our hands are frozen.

-Irregular Heartbeats (Tachycardia or Extrasystole)

The vagus nerve slows the heartbeat. If it didn't exist, the heart would beat out of control.

Clearly, if we have a poorly functioning vagus nerve, it is easier to have episodes of tachycardia or extrasystole.

-Inflammation and Other Symptoms

As we have seen, the vagus nerve is an anti-inflammatory system: those who have a poorly functioning vagus nerve tend to have frequent inflammations at various levels.

The electrical stimulation of the vagus nerve has been used, with very encouraging results, in the treatment of the inflammatory disease par excellence, that is, rheumatoid arthritis: this has helped experts realize the anti-inflammatory power of the vagus nerve and the consequent problems if it does not work.

There are also a whole other series of symptoms such as:
- paleness
- excessive sweating
- neck stiffness
- cervical pain
- swallowing difficulties
- "knotty throat" sensation
- insensitivity or unilateral tingling of the scalp
- obesity
- anxiety
- mood disorders

Of course, most of the conditions described above can lead to other diseases; for example obesity and inflammation are both linked to cancer and diabetes. Anxiety or mood disorders can also lead to depression. Your vagus nerve has a significant role in everybody's overall wellbeing and performance.

-Gastroparesis

Gastroparesis is a chronic medical condition, which consists of partial paralysis of the stomach.

The onset of gastroparesis causes the ingested food to remain in the stomach for a long time; in other words, the stomach of people suffering from gastroparesis does not empty at the same speed as in healthy people, but does so more slowly; therefore, the digestive process it assists is slowed down.

It is generally the condition of the vagus nerve which determines the state of gastroparesis is, in general. As stated, the vagus nerve is the nervous structure which, inducing the contraction of the muscular wall of the stomach, regulates the transit of food from the gastric compartment to the intestine.

GASTROPARESIS

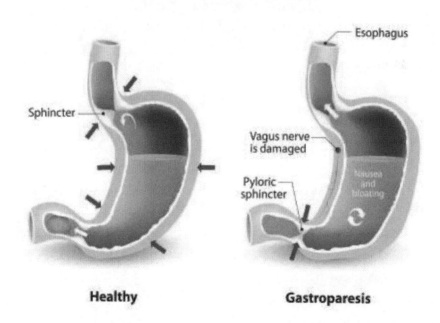

TYPICAL SYMPTOMS OF GASTROPARESIS ARE:

- Immediate feeling of satiety, even after small meals
- Nausea and vomiting
- Loss of appetite
- Weight loss
- Sense of swelling in the stomach
- Abdominal pain and discomfort
- Heartburn

The intensity of symptoms varies from patient to patient. In fact, some individuals with gastroparesis complain of unbearable ailments, while others experience discomfort that is much less acute and with which they can live normally.

Moreover, it is quite frequent that the above-mentioned manifestations are inconstant, i.e. they are present at certain times of the day and absent at others.

COMPLICATIONS

In the absence of any treatment and in the most serious patients, gastroparesis can lead to several complications, some of which are also very dangerous.

Possible complications include:

- Dehydration.
  This is due to continuous episodes of vomiting.
- Gastroesophageal reflux disease.
  This is when the acid content of the stomach rises chronically in the oesophagus and progressively damages it.
- Malnutrition.
  This is a consequence of poor appetite, repeated vomiting, feeling full even after small meals and frequent heartburn.
- Abnormal fluctuations in blood glucose levels.
  This is the result of slow digestion and represents an

important danger for diabetics.
- Tiredness and weight loss
- Bowel obstruction.
    This is a very dangerous condition, which requires immediate medical intervention.
- Bacterial infections.
    This is the result of food remaining in the stomach for a long time.

There are several tests you can undergo, under the supervision and treatment of a doctor.

The purpose of these tests is to rule out other potential illnesses with similar symptoms.

Some of the common tests used to diagnose gastroparesis include:

• Gastric emptying study
• Upper gastrointestinal endoscopy
• Ultrasound
• Upper gastrointestinal series

Gastric Emptying Study
The process of the gastric emptying study includes some of the most important information in making a gastroparesis diagnosis. Your medical professional will instruct you to eat a small meal, like an egg or two with a piece of toast, along with a little bit of radioactive material. Then a scanner is used to watch the movement of this radioactive
material in your body. It is placed on your abdomen to watch the rate of food removal from your stomach. If you are taking medication that can slow down stomach emptying, you will need to interrupt it for the study. If you are unsure as to whether your medication interferes with this, you should ask your medical professional about it.

Upper Gastrointestinal Endoscopy
The upper GI, or gastrointestinal, endoscopy requires the use

of a camera on a long tube to examine the digestive tract. It goes through your esophagus, stomach, and the upper part of your small intestine, also called the duodenum. This test is also used to diagnose other conditions like pyloric stenosis and peptic ulcer disease. The symptoms of these diseases can be similar to the symptoms of gastroparesis.

Ultrasounds

Ultrasounds are great tests for producing images of your internal body without entering it with radioactive materials or cameras on tubing. It uses sound waves that operate at a high frequency to create the images. This test is used to help diagnose problems with your kidneys or gallbladder, which could also be causing your symptoms.

X-Rays

Another test that occurs outside the body are x-rays of your digestive tract; however, most often for testing for gastroparesis, your medical professional will require you to drink a liquid that is chalky and white, called barium, which coats your digestive tract to highlight any abnormalities in the x-ray.

The best way to treat this dysfunction is to recognize the condition causing it and treat that. For example, if diabetes is causing it, you need to treat and control your diabetes. If it is caused by damage to your vagus nerve, you should treat and stimulate your nerve.

THE VAGUS NERVE AND FAINTING

Vasovagal syndrome (sometimes called vasovagal crisis) is a type of syncope (fainting) belonging to the group of neuro-mediated syncopes. Syncope is an abrupt, but transient, loss of consciousness caused by a reduction in blood pressure, such as to cause a reduction in blood flow to the brain.

Fainting is transient and followed by a total, rapid and spontaneous recovery.

Vascular-vagal syncope is the most common form of syncope in healthy people. It is caused by a vagus-mediated neurogenic mechanism that can be triggered by various stimuli, the most common of which are :

- emotional, like anxiety, stress, fear or intense pain
- heat exposure
- sight of blood (or blood sample)
- excessive effort during evacuation (but also coughing, sneezing, laughing, ...)
- staying in an upright position for a long time

Over-stimulation of the vagus by these stimuli leads to a sudden drop in pressure due to dilation of blood vessels accompanied by a slower heartbeat (bradycardia); these two mechanisms are responsible for a decrease in blood flow to the brain and subsequent temporary fainting.

The vasovagal syndrome can be clinically divided into two stages:

1.   Prodromal Period
2.   Fainting

1. The prodromal period, which precedes the loss of consciousness, is characterized by the following symptoms:
  -    paleness

- cold sweats
- fattening tiredness
- dizziness
- tinnitus
- nausea
- vision impairment

The patient may start yawning and feel the need to expose himself to fresh air or to go to the bathroom; as the pressure decreases, the vision may become blurred, with the appearance of black spots.

2. The prodromal phase is usually followed by fainting (if this is not the case we do not talk about syncope, but lipotomy), during which it is possible to detect:
- jerky movements
- slow and weak pulse
- dilated pupils.

Recovery usually occurs in less than a minute, but it is important that the patient get up very gradually to avoid further loss of consciousness.

The vasovagal syndrome does not affect the brain system, but it must be treated because of the high risk of falls.

If a person does not faint frequently, the vasovagal syncope need not be treated.

EXERCISES AND TECHNIQUES TO ACTIVATE YOUR VAGUS NERVE

When you know how to regulate and heal your vagus nerve you can help yourself reduce chronic inflammation, overcome migraines, reduce symptoms of chronic auto-immune disease, depression, and anxiety. Thankfully, in most cases now, you can learn how to regulate this nerve on your own without the intervention of a medical professional.

HOW TO STIMULATE THE VAGUS NERVE NATURALLY

There are different strategies for invigorating the vagus nerve to help support your wellbeing:

1. Expose Yourself to The Cold

Cold can stimulate the vagus nerve and the digestive system. "Cold exposure, like taking a cold shower or soaking the face, also stimulates the nerves," says Mentore. Studies show that when your body adapts to the cold, your fight or flight system (sympathetic system) decreases and your resting and digestive system (parasympathetic system) increases; this is mediated by the vagus nerve. Any type of acute exposure to cold (splashing cold water on your face; drinking ice water; dipping your face in cold water; putting ice cubes in a zip pocket and holding the ice against your face whilst holding your breath for a moment; immersing the tongue in a liquid) increases the activation of the vagus nerve. Try to finish your next shower with at least 30 seconds of cold water and see how you feel.

Remember to consult your doctor first. Most doctors advise

against taking cold showers in the case of people with cardiac disorders. This is because sudden exposure to cold can restrict blood vessels, which can increase heart rate and blood pressure.

2. Singing and Chanting

Singing, whether it be mantras, hymns or energetic singing, causes an increased heart rate variability (HRV) in slightly different ways. Basically, singing triggers a vagus pump that sends out relaxing waves, improves resilience and causes better adaptation to stress. Singing at the top of your lungs makes the muscles in your throat activate the vagus. Singing in unison, which is often practiced in churches and synagogues, also increases HRV and wave function. Singing has been proved to increase oxytocin, also known as the love hormone, because it brings people closer together.

3. Gargling and Chewing

Another home remedy for an under-stimulated vagus nerve is gargling with water. Gargling actually stimulates the muscles of the paddle that are pulled by the vagus nerve. Theoretically, gargling contracts these muscles, which can activate the vagus nerve and stimulate the gastrointestinal tract.

Chewing also stimulates the activity of the vagus nerve and the parasympathetic system that activates digestion. This means that while chewing gum can have disadvantages, it also stimulates the vagus nerve.

4. Exercise

Exercise is an integral part of a healthy lifestyle. But it also seems to be useful to stimulate the vagus nerve. This may be the reason why exercise helps us to relax.

Exercise refines your brain's growth hormone, supports your brain's mitochondria, and helps reduce the rate of cognitive decline. However, it has also been shown to stimulate the vagus nerve, which has a positive effect on the brain and mental health. Light training also stimulates intestinal flow, which is mediated by the vagus nerve. You should choose an activity you enjoy so that you do it consistently.

5. Cough or Strain the Abdominal Muscles

If you push down (as with bowel movements), you can successfully stimulate your vagus nerve mechanically. Some even say that's why people feel relaxed after a bowel movement.

6. Massage/ Reflexology

There are certain areas on your body that connect to your Vagus nerve more superficially. This means that you can access this Vagus nerve easier from the outside of your body.

The carotid sinus, tucked in your neck, is known to help stimulate your Vagus nerve. It is easily accessible during a massage. It is known to help prevent and reduce seizures in patients.

You can invigorate your vagus nerve by massaging your feet. A foot massage can lower your heart rate and blood pressure. All of these benefits are known to lower the risk of developing heart disease.

Using mild and firm pressure during a massage can help stimulate the Vagus nerve. Infant massage is a common therapy parents and caregivers can use to help a baby gain weight. The process stimulates the digestive process, which is regulated and controlled by the Vagus nerve.

7. Laughter

Happiness and laughter are simple immune enhancers, as well as a great way to relax. The saying "laughter is the best medicine" can contain a truth. A study from 2013 came to an interesting conclusion: there is a connection between physical health, emotional health and social pleasure. Positive social interactions affect positive emotions, which improves vagal tone. This then enhanced physical health.

However, studies are still scarce and it is difficult to say how and why we feel so good with laughter. A study of laughing in yoga showed an increase in HRV (heart rate variability) in the laughing group. Also, activation of the Vagus nerve can result in laughter. There are many benefits to laughter in addition to stimulating the Vagus nerve, including lowering the risk of heart disease, improving cognitive functioning, and increasing beta-endorphins.

8.Prayer

Researchers found that prayer enhanced the rhythm of the heart, improving the resting heart rate as well as the heart rate variability. One observation unique to the study on this reciting the rosary prayer was that the prayer took ten seconds to recite, meaning the participants had to take a breath that lasted for ten seconds, resulting in an average of about six breaths per minute; breathing at this slow rate increases your heart rate variability, thereby activating your Vagus nerve.

9. Buzzing/ Humming

The vagus nerve goes through the vocal cords and inner ear, and the buzzing vibrations are a free and easy way to affect your nervous system. Choose your favourite song or, if yoga is more your thing, you can 'OM' your way to well-being. Notice and appreciate the sensations in your chest, neck and head.

10. Positive Social Relationships

Healthy connections to others- in person, on the phone, via social media- can activate the regulation of our bodies and minds. Relationships show the spirit of playfulness and creativity, and help us to relax in a relationship based on mutual trust.

A study encouraged participants to think compassionately about others, while quietly repeating positive sentences about their friends and family. The meditators have shown an overall increase in positive emotions such as serenity, joy and hope after completing the course. These positive thoughts from others led to an improvement in vagus function, which was reflected in the variability in heart rate.

11. **Acupuncture**

The ancient treatment of acupuncture in Chinese medicine can be helpful in stimulating the vagus nerve. According to traditional acupuncture points, your ears can be particularly stimulating.

Research shows that ear acupuncture can have the following advantages:

- Cardiovascular regulation
- Respiratory regulation
- Regulation of the gastrointestinal tract

But make sure you work with a qualified acupuncturist and tell your doctor if you plan to use acupuncture, as it can be dangerous.

12. **Coffee Enemas**

Enemas are like activations for your vagus nerve. The enlargement of the intestine increases the activation of the vagus nerve, as is the case with enemas. This cleansing is achieved by the liver being able to detoxify toxins in the blood and bind them to the bile. During this process, the liver cleanses itself by releasing the toxic bile in the small intestine, and then in the large intestine that are to be evacuated. The entire blood supply circulates in the liver every three minutes. If the coffee is kept inside for 12 to 15 minutes, the blood will circulate four to five times for cleaning, similar to a dialysis treatment. The water content of coffee stimulates the intestinal peristalsis and helps to empty the colon with the accumulated toxic bile.

13. **Nervana**

This portable product sends a gentle electrical wave through the left ear canal, to stimulate the body's vagus nerve while synchronizing with the music. In turn, this stimulates the release of neurotransmitters in the brain, which create sensations beneficial for the whole body.

14. Relaxing

Learning to relax can be the most important thing to keep your vagus nerve fit. Reading a book, listening to cool music, or playing - it doesn't matter what you do, but take the time to do it.

15. Shaft Vibration

The scientific community has extensively studied wave vibration for its health benefits. This therapy consists of standing on a vibrating plate that generates low vibrations. These vibrations then create decisive stress throughout the body (like the kind of stress that comes from training). This stress activates the vagus nerve between other parts of the body.

16. Zinc

Zinc is a common mineral in supplements and in foods, but amazingly many humans do not consume enough of it. In a study where rats were given a diet low or deficient in zinc for 3 days, it was clear the vagus nerve was not functioning at full capacity. When zinc was reintroduced the vagus nerve was activated and stimulated

17. Healthy Fats and Omega-3

They are mainly found in fish and are necessary for the normal electrical function of your nervous system. They affect the brain, mental health and many aspects of wellbeing. They have been shown to help people overcome addiction, repair a "leaky brain", and even reverse cognitive decline.

Researchers also found that omega-3 fatty acids increase vagal tone and activity. Studies have shown that they lower heart rate and increase heart rate variability, which means they stimulate the vagus nerve.

A study published in *Frontiers of Psychology* in 2011 found that high fish consumption was associated with a predominantly parasympathetic (relaxed) nervous system and increased vagal activity. The researchers assumed that the Omega-3 content in the fish was the reason.

18.Get Out in the Sunshine

It may sound counter-intuitive given what we know about the harmful rays of the sun and our skin; however, the sun is a good source of MSH or Alpha-MSH. In studies on rats, an introduction of Alpha-MSH helped lower the risk of stroke because of the lowering of inflammation and the activation of the vagus nerve.

VAGUS NERVE STIMULATION EXERCISES

BREATHING EXERCISES

Breathing techniques are one of the most effective ways to switch from the sympathetic nervous system to the parasympathetic nervous system that activates rest and relaxation responses.

The key to deep breathing techniques is to feel the motions of inhaling and exhaling in your upper belly rather than in the chest area. Effective breathing, when it comes to stimulation of the vagus nerve, should also focus on reducing the number of breaths taken per minute and extending exhalation.

Breathe Deeply and Slowly

Breathing is one of the fastest ways to affect the states of our nervous system. Your heart and neck contain neurons with receptors called baroreceptors, that measure blood pressure and send the neuronal signal to your brain. This activates your vagus nerve, which connects to your heart to lower blood pressure and heart rate. The result is less activation of fight or flight (sympathetic nervous system) and greater activity of rest and digestion (parasympathetic nervous system).

The goal is to move your stomach and diaphragm with your breath in order to slow your breathing. Vagus nerve stimulation occurs when breathing is slowed down from our typical 10-14 breaths per minute, to 5-7 breaths per minute. Slow breathing, with roughly the same inhalation and exhalation duration, increases the sensitivity of the baroreceptors and vagal activation. Strengthening this part of your nervous system can have significant benefits.

When you breathe slowly and deeply, your vagus nerve is

activated. It sends soothing signals that slow down your brain waves and heart rate and set in motion all the rest and repair mechanisms that are responsible for your body's natural relaxation response.

Therefore, slow, deep breathing is vital. But there is a problem. Living in a constant stress mode promotes a restricted, fast and shallow breathing pattern. Slow and deep breathing can take a little practice.

When you breathe, you need to use your diaphragm. The diaphragm is your most important respiratory muscle. It is bell-shaped and should flatten when inhaled, as it acts like a piston and creates a vacuum in your chest cavity, allowing your lungs to expand and air to enter.

On the other hand, it creates pressure, pushes the bowels down and out, and enlarges your belly. Therefore, good breathing practice is called abdominal breathing.

A Simple Deep Breathing Process

1. Lie back and close your eyes slightly. Place your hands above the lower part of your abdomen.
2. Take a deep breath with the diaphragm (abdominal breathing). It is the basis for good breathing and for the relief of anxiety. When you inhale, let your lower abdomen rise gently as if it were filling your breath.
3. When you exhale, let your lower abdomen relax as if it were emptying.
4. Continue with a nice, light rhythm that easily follows your breath as your stomach moves slowly up and down. See if it is possible not to force it, because it should be natural, easy and effortless.

Use this calming rhythm for a few minutes and then pay attention to how good you feel.

You should practice this simple deep breathing meditation once a day, to relieve everyday stress and the accumulated layers of tension from the past. You can do this while lying in bed at night before you sleep, to prepare your body for a deep break. In no time you will have restored your body's natural balance, which leads to a more balanced, happier and peaceful life.

Breathe with the Glottis Partially Closed

The glottis is on the back of your tongue and is closed when you hold your breath. Here we want it to be partially closed. It is the feeling in your throat when you exhale and make an "hhhhh" sound to clean your glasses. It is similar to when you are drifting off to sleep and you are about to snore a little.

By controlling the glottis, you are achieving the following:

1. Airflow control during both inhalation and exhalation
2. Stimulation of your vagus nerve.

Now is the time to put this whole theory into practice using this diaphragmatic breathing technique.

1. Breathe in through your nose using your diaphragm, the glottis is partially closed, as if you were making a "hhhhh" sound.
2. Hold your breath for a moment
3. Exhale through your nose (or mouth), with the glottis partially closed, as if you were almost making a "hhhhh" sound.
4. It is a breathing cycle, so complete between 6 to 12 cycles to see the results.

The more you practise, the more effective this technique becomes. When your newly acquired breathability is established and abdominal breathing becomes a habit, you will find that your body is constantly working at a much lower stress level.

You will also notice how your breathing responds to stressful situations. Your body is conditioned to automatically control your breathing and thus your stress and anxiety. One of the secrets to dealing with anxiety is learning how to stimulate your vagus nerve by breathing properly. The vagus nerve acts as a mind-body connection and controls your relaxation reaction. You can stimulate your vagus nerve by utilizing diaphragmatic breathing with the glottis partially closed. Use your free time to consistently practice this technique, put it into practice, and you will be amazed by the results.

VALSALVA MANEUVER

The Valsalva Maneuver is a respiratory maneuver which consists of performing a forced exhalation with the glottis closed. The Valsalva manoeuvre is performed by inhaling deeply and then exhaling forcefully, with the mouth closed and the nose plugged to prevent the air from escaping. This causes an increase in air pressure in the chest and middle ear.

This is one of the vagal maneuvers used to stop tachycardias, as it helps to trigger the vagal reflex, which slows the heart rate at the level of the atria.

How to carry out the Valsalva maneuver:

- Pinch your nose shut. Close your mouth.
- Try to breathe out, as though blowing up a balloon.
- Do this for around 10 to 15 seconds.

The Valsalva maneuver should be possible sitting or resting. Ask your therapeutic expert which approach is right for you.

This is be a fast and simple method to get your heart beating at a safe and normal rate if you're able to do it safely. Go ahead and ask if your doctor has never recommended it. Turns out, it might be a great aid to your heart and your quality of life.

MEDITATION

Numerous studies claim that meditating increases parasympathetic activity of the nervous system which, in turn, improves vagal tone.

The objective of meditation is to be able to focus attention on ourselves, following perceptions, sensations, thoughts and emotions, or on the external environment, in order to reach a level of greater awareness and inner calmness.

Benefits of Meditation

Meditation is a discipline with ancient origins, but it is becoming more and more topical and, if practiced with constancy, it can bring innumerable advantages. Here are 7 benefits from it:

1. It's a natural remedy for anxiety and depression.
2. It helps to regain psychophysical well-being: it has a very restful effect and is an important tool to better

understand yourself and your limits.
3. It improves memory and concentration.
4. It relieves stress and increases productivity at work.
5. It helps to reduce physical pain without any side effects, unlike drugs.
6. Lowers blood pressure: meditation promotes the release of nitric oxide into the blood, a substance able to relax blood vessels allowing the blood to flow better. Combining meditation with a healthy and balanced diet and constant physical activity is an excellent natural remedy against high blood pressure.
7. Keeps you young: meditation slows down the aging process of cells.

How to Meditate

Find the Time

Learning to meditate is not easy. It requires energy, tenacity and regularity. Above all, it takes time.

So, anyone who wants to approach meditation must necessarily find time for themselves.

The first thing you need to do is to isolate yourself in the course of your day for 10 minutes. It really begins gradually. It's the only way to make sure you get the practice going. Then, if you want to, you can increase your sitting time. But don't be in a hurry or have performance anxiety. In meditation there's nothing to prove to anyone.

The ideal would be in the morning, but let's be clear; we must reconcile meditation with daily life... work, family, love, friends, commitments and entertainment are all important and essential parts of our daily routine. But it is enough to find 10 minutes for yourself, exclusively yours, to make a difference. No phone, no doorbells, no people calling you. You don't exist for the world in those minutes, you're only there for yourself.

Set A Timer

Our mind is constantly moving. It often goes from one thought to another at the speed of light and seems to have no peace. If you don't use a timer, it is likely that your thought will often go in this direction: 'When does this meditation end?'. If, on the other hand, you know that after the set time an alarm clock will sound and take you back to your normal activities, you will have found a way to "keep your mind quiet".

Find Your Place

At some point in your life, you will surely have come into a place and felt immediately comfortable, or vice versa a place you want to leave as soon as possible.

Meditating means relaxing your mind and feeling good, so it is essential that this happens in a place where you feel safe and comfortable. It doesn't matter if it is a room of one square meter or if you are on top of a mountain with infinity around you.

What you will discover with these exercises is meditation in your daily life, so you can easily build your place in your own home.

It may be a corner of the bedroom, it may be the living room, it may even be the laundry room if you use this space in the right way.

Do you like oriental colors and fabrics? Well, you'll just need to get some pillows and curtains of colored fabric.

Do you prefer a sober white colour with very few colour elements? Cover the sofa with a white blanket or sheet. You can create the atmosphere you prefer, also helping with fragrances and essential oils.

Find Your Location

When we imagine someone meditating, we see them in the classic "lotus flower" position and the first thing we think is "How can I cross my legs like this and stay there for 10 minutes?".

The good news is that you don't even have to try it at first, unless you are already used to yoga or gymnastic exercises that make you particularly flexible in your hips. Because in the end, instead of letting yourself go into meditation, you would waste your energy just trying to maintain the perfect position.

In order to be able to meditate, your position must necessarily be comfortable, bearing in mind some basic rules.

Keep your mind alert (in other words, you have to meditate and not fall asleep) so keep your spine upright, your knees slightly lower than your pelvis and your head slightly forward.

This position can be achieved by sitting on the floor, perhaps using a support, but even on a chair it will be fine. Just make sure you keep your back upright but not rigid and do not lean against the backrest, otherwise you may gradually risk bending forward.

Meditation Exercises

1st EXERCISE

Conscious Breathing

Focus on breathing to feel the air coming in and out of your nostrils. It is easy to be distracted by thoughts, so our goal will be to ignore them to the point of weakening them.

When a thought arrives (and it is inevitable that it will arrive), as soon as you realize that your mind is "following" it, it should go back to concentrating on breathing.

2nd EXERCISE

Counting Backwards

This technique is very simple and very useful during meditation. With our eyes closed, we count backwards starting from high numbers, like 50 or 100, to zero.

The objective is to concentrate on a single thought/activity, in order to eliminate the sensations produced by other stimuli.

3rd EXERCISE

Scanning the Body

In this meditation exercise you have to use your mind to make a complete "scan" of your body. Start from the top of your hair, scalp, forehead, face, whole body to your feet. Feel the body and perceive the resulting sensations (heat, tingling, pressure, pain). You can contract and relax the various muscle groups to be aware of their presence and movement.

It is an interesting way to observe and perceive the sensations of our body in detail.

If you perceive other thoughts let them go without following them; they will disappear after a while.

4th EXERCISE

Dynamic Observation

Adopt a comfortable position, preferably seated, and keep your eyes closed. Afterwards, open them for a moment and close them again. Finally, try to reflect on what you have seen.

This observation exercise helps us to analyze the different sensations produced by visual stimuli. We can enumerate them, think about the shape, colour or name of each object.

Meditation in Everyday Life

Every activity, if carried out in a conscious and non-judgmental way, can be considered a form of meditation. For example, daily activities such as brushing your teeth, setting the table, taking a shower, opening a door, can become practical meditation exercises to train our awareness.

Here is an example of a meditation exercise to do at home daily and in a simple way.

- Turn the Shower into A Form of Meditation

In order for a habitual action such as "taking a shower" to become a form of meditation, you must learn not to do it 'automatically' but to pay attention to everything you perceive with your 5 senses. This is how:

Use Touch: Feel the sensation of cold metal under your fingertips when you turn on the faucet, feel the warmth of the water flowing on your skin and the smooth surface under your feet inside the shower.

- Use your sense of smell: what is the smell of your shower gel? Try to feel the difference between when you smell it inside the container and when you smell it on your skin.
- Use Your Hearing: What is the sound of running water? What feelings does it give you?
- Use Taste: just before you start showering, or as soon as you finish, try drinking a glass of water. What does it taste like? Have you ever thought about it?
- Sight is often one of the senses we use the most. To give more space to smell, hearing, touch and taste, try closing your eyes while taking a shower. Inevitably, the other sensations will seem more vivid.

- Another little 'trick' to turn every activity into a 'little meditation' is to slow down the rhythm a bit. When you do things more calmly, you can notice more all the aspects that you would overlook if you move 'in automatic mode'.

OM CHANTING

Various studies have shown that OM chanting deactivates the limbic part of the brain responsible for our basic emotions (fear, pleasure, anger) and our impulses (hunger, sex, dominance and care of offspring).

Since the effectiveness of OM chanting is associated with the experience of vibrations around the ears, scientists have suggested that these sensations are transmitted through the auricular branch of the vagus nerve.

As the vagus nerve branches off into the inner ear and larynx, controlling the opening and closing of the vocal cords and tone of the sound, it appears that this is stimulated during the vocalization of the O and M sounds. In addition, by performing chanting in exhalation, the vagus nerve is activated in its role as manager of the parasympathetic system. In addition, chanting, by facilitating the lengthening of the exhalation, further amplifies the effect on the parasympathetic system. This is why this practice helps to calm and relax the body and mind.

-Find a quiet place to sit comfortably.

-A good position is to sit with your legs crossed and your back straight.

-Wear comfortable cotton clothes that do not tighten any part of your body. All body channels should be free and comfortable.

1. Place the palm of your right hand (facing upwards) on the palm of your left hand at navel level.
2. Close your eyes for a few minutes and relax your mind and body.
   Slowly feel the vibrations that occur in every part of your body.

3. When the vibrations become more intense, start breathing deeply.
4. Hold your breath for a second and then slowly exhale. Initially count to 7 as you exhale.
5. This ought to be duplicated thrice.
6. As you exhale the third time, sing "ooooooooooo..." Feel the vibrations in your abdomen (and under your chest).
7. After exhaling, relax for 2 seconds.
8. Breathe in again (slow, deep breaths). As you exhale sing "ooooo..." and feel the vibrations in your chest and neck.
9. After exhaling, relax for 2 seconds.
10. Inhale again (long, deep breath). As you exhale, sing "mmmmmmmm...". Feel the vibrations in your head and neck.
11. After exhaling, relax for 2 seconds.
12. Inhale again and as you exhale say "oooommmm..." or "aaauuummm...". About 80% of the sound should be "aaauuu..." and 20% should be "mmmm...".
13. Repeat the previous steps 3 times (you can do it up to 9 times).
14. After the Om meditation, relax and concentrate on your regular breathing for about 5 minutes.

TIPS

-Wearing white clothes and being in a white environment will improve your experience. But the rule of white is not fundamental.

-A good place could be a quiet room or a garden with shade. Your eyes, ears or other sensory organs should not be disturbed.

-Do not consume alcohol for at least 8-10 hours before meditation.

-It would be better not to eat or drink anything for at least 2 hours before meditation. The body's channels should not be blocked in order to achieve maximum results. This applies especially to the digestive system.

-The best times for this meditation are early in the morning or late at night.

-For beginners, singing "aum" can cause dizziness. It is recommended to proceed slowly and try to learn one step at a time. In this way you will prepare body and mind for the next step.

-It is very important to open your eyes slowly when your breathing has stabilized.

-If you cannot sit on the floor, you can try sitting on a bed or a chair. The most important thing is to keep your back straight.

-Doing this kind of meditation in a group brings more peace and harmony to all members than doing it alone.

YOGA

Yoga is a combination of physical, mental, and spiritual exercises that utilizes breathing techniques, exercises, and meditation. The main aim of yoga exercises is to achieve harmony in the body, mind, and environment.

When it comes to increasing your vagal tone, the role of yoga is to increase the flexibility not just of your body but also of your autonomic nervous system. Yoga can help you in learning how to switch from your sympathetic to parasympathetic systems by mastering stress and recovering from trauma. By following yoga practices, you will be able to boost your vagal tone and activate your parasympathetic responses.

9 Yoga Poses for Beginners

Yoga is not gymnastics, but a real discipline. This does not detract from the fact that, to begin with, you can practice some of the simplest positions, combining slow breathing and trying to feel the energy flow through your body. Here are a few to get you started:

1.Sukhasana, or literally, Easy Position.

Achieve this position by sitting with your legs stretched out, stretching the spine before bending the legs and putting the feet under the opposite knees. Start by staying in position for a minute, then gradually increase the time.

Benefits:
-Relieves tension in the back
-Promotes meditation
-Reduces stress and anxiety levels
-Improves posture
-Promotes better breathing

2.Balasana, the Baby's Position.

This is a perfect position if you suffer from back pain, and that has a great relaxing power. Start with your knees on the floor on the mat and your pelvis on them, with your hands resting shoulder wide, and your shoulders in line. Join your toes, and back with the weight of your hips, sit on your heels. Rest your buttocks on them. Let go of the torso, and rest your forehead down to the ground, if you can; if not just go as far as you can.

Benefits:
-Reduces stress and fatigue
-Extends ankles, hips and thighs
-Relieves cervical pain
-Relieves back pain

3.Marjariasana, the Position of the Cat.

Begin by getting down on all fours, with your hands at the same height and distance of the shoulders, and knees at the hips. When you inhale deeply, arch your back, pushing it downwards, raising your torso and holding your chin up with your eyes upwards. When you exhale, straighten your back and make a hump with your spine, just like a cat. The head goes down, looking down at the navel. The position repeats itself and follows the rhythm of your breathing. You can repeat it as many times as you want, it will give you great benefit throughout the entire back area.

Benefits:
-Gives relief to the back and belly.
-Stimulates the kidneys and adrenal glands
-Makes movements more flexible
-Prevents back pain
-It relieves cervical pains

4.Adho Mukha Svanasana, Upside Down Dog.

Starting from the cat position, straighten your elbows and push your palms to the ground, distributing the weight between your hands and feet. Exhale and lift your knees off the ground, trying to raise the ischi as much as possible and stretch the coccyx. Try to stretch your legs as far as possible, driving your heels into the ground. Start by holding this position for five breaths.

Benefits:
-Relieves back pain.
-Energizes the whole body
-Strengthens legs and arms
-Promotes digestion
-Prevents osteoporosis
-Helps to relieve symptoms of asthma and sinusitis
-Helps in the treatment of depression

5.Tadasana, the Location of the Mountain.

To practice this yoga position, stand with your heels and toes together, and the whole base of the foot touching the ground. Then try to move your weight back and forth, raising your heels and toes each time, and then left and right. Once you have found your center, contract the quadriceps and raise the kneecaps, with the coccyx going down and the pubis towards the navel. Keep your stomach in, shoulders open, back stretched and neck straight. You choose how to hold your arms and stay balanced. Hold that position for 30 seconds at first, and then double the time you stay in this position every time you practice.

Benefits:
-Improves posture.
-Balances the first chakra
-Tones buttocks and strengthens the thighs, knees and ankles
-Helps with balance, teaching us how to better distribute our weight

6. Phalakasana or Plank Pose

Start by kneeling on all fours above the mat with hands aligned and wrists under the shoulders. Stretch one leg backwards and root all toes on the ground. Do the same with the second leg. Then extend your heels backwards, point your toes firmly into the ground and flex your legs firmly, pushing your thighs upwards. Stretch out your arms well and stretch your neck forward. Be careful not to bend your back and not to bend your arms or bottom to the ground. Tighten your abdomen and buttocks. Stay in position for a couple of minutes.

Benefits:
- Relieves insomnia, migraine, menopause and osteoporosis. It also reduces stress.
- Regular practice of this asana creates new bone tissue. This strengthens your bones and makes them healthier.
- It also makes your spine strong, thus improving your posture.
- It helps to develop mental endurance. It allows you to continue to challenge yourself.

7. Purvottanasana

Sit on the floor with your legs stretched out in front of you. Place your hands next to your buttocks with your palms facing the ground. Move your hands backwards, resting them about 10 centimeters away from your back, always with palms on the ground and fingertips facing forward.

Bend your knees and place the soles of your feet on the ground with your toes facing inwards.

Exhale and, pressing down with the palms of your hands and the soles of your feet, lift your pelvis off the ground, trying to keep your chest and thighs parallel to the ground and arms and calves perpendicular to the ground, as if your body formed the figure of a table with four legs.

Now, without lowering your pelvis, stretch your legs one at a time. Lift your pelvis up a little more, without tightening the muscles of your buttocks too much.

Bring the shoulder blades closer together to support the raised chest. Without squeezing the back of the neck, slowly lower the head backwards.

This is the final position. Hold it until you can balance effort and relaxation, breathing normally.

Breathe out and slowly return to the starting position.

Benefits:

- Stretches all the muscles in the front of your body.
- Fortifies back, arms, wrists and legs.
- Strengthens the joints of the shoulders, chest and ankles.
- Stimulates the nervous system.
- It widens the chest and relaxes the lungs.
- Improves posture by training the shoulders, chest and upper abdominal muscles.

8. Vasisthasana

You should have a lot of experience before attempting this position. It is not recommended for those with joint or muscle problems in the arms, shoulders and wrists.

To perform the simplest version of this posture, place the palms of your hands on the yoga mat while your legs are stretched out. With conscious attention, rotate the body sideways, in order to leave the palm of the hand (right or left, depending on the twist) and the side of the right or left foot (the other foot should be lying on the foot in contact with the mat) resting on the ground. If it is the right hand that is resting on the ground, lift the left arm vertically in line with the right arm. The back and legs should be well aligned. In this version the legs stay in contact with each other.

Benefits:
- It tones the entire upper part of the body and

strengthens the back muscles, especially the lumbar area.
- Increases mobility of hip joints.
- Develops balance and concentration.
- Develops sustainability in life
- Develop a state of satisfaction and happiness.

9. Anantasana

Grab your left knee, bringing it closer to your armpit and grab your big toe with the fingers of your left hand, middle and large index finger. Move the left side of the pelvis forward towards the inner thigh and slowly straighten the leg. Press the big toe against the fingers and stretch the left leg upwards, starting this movement from the middle of the hip joint. Continue to pull the right leg, pushing the heel away from you, retract the sacrum and shoulder blades, directing them toward the front surface of the body. The navel, on the contrary, should be directed to the spine.

To relax from this position, bend your left knee and roll onto your back. Repeat on the other side.

Benefits

- Tones the abdominal muscles, thus improving digestion.
- Tones the back thigh muscles
- Makes the spine more flexible
- Helps to treat hypertension, arthritis, colitis,

hypertension, and sciatica.
- Helps to relieve stress and tension.

DIET CHANGES TO STIMULATE THE VAGUS NERVE

One way you may begin to help your vagus nerve is through changing your diet. Remember, your vagus nerve travels down to your guts. It is directly influenced by the hormone levels that are produced there. It can also help heal and send better messages up to the brain if you provide it the nutritional support that it needs. This means that changing up your diet may help your vagus nerve to become more effective in general.

The Mediterranean diet is a great way to help your vagus nerve.

THE MEDITERRANEAN DIET

This is a dietary model that is characterized by its variety, in addition to a strong nutritional balance, provides for the consumption of all foods, without any exclusion: it suggests a high consumption of vegetables, legumes, fresh and dried fruit, olive oil and whole grains; a moderate consumption of fish, dairy products (especially cheese and yogurt), meat and a low consumption of sweets.

It has been scientifically proven to improve health, increasing protection against the most common chronic diseases, such as hypertension, diabetes, obesity and cancer, reducing the onset of cardiovascular disease and preventing neurodegenerative diseases, such as Alzheimer's and Parkinson's disease. By now all the most important and influential scientific societies consider it as the ideal dietary style to preserve health and to reduce the onset of the most important chronic diseases. The way to maintain a healthy balance is precisely to follow a varied diet, which includes foods from all food groups, because only in this way you can assemble the complex puzzle of nutrients and protective substances essential in keeping the body healthy.

The main characteristics of Mediterranean cuisine are:

- A high consumption of vegetables, fruit (including nuts), legumes and cereals
- Extra virgin olive oil as a privileged condiment fat
- Moderate consumption of fish, meat, cheese and yoghurt
- An active lifestyle

MEDITERRANEAN DIET

FOODS TO EAT EVERY DAY

The following foods are essential in keeping the body healthy, and should ideally be eaten every day:

Cereals:

bread, pasta, rice but also barley, spelt and tubers such as potatoes. They provide mainly carbohydrates (primary source of energy for the body), but also B vitamins (useful for transforming energy in cells) and proteins (the building blocks of the body's tissues).

Often choosing bread or whole grains guarantees the body, in addition to the nutrients just listed, the optimal amount of dietary fiber (essential for the intestines and to prevent eating excessively).

Recommended servings: 2-3 portions per day

Fruit and Vegetables:

are considered essential foods in the Mediterranean diet to maintain health and fitness because they provide fiber, β-carotene (carrots, peppers, tomatoes, apricots, melons, etc.), a precursor of vitamin A, useful for vision, immune system function and cell growth, vitamin C (citrus fruits, strawberries, kiwis, tomatoes, peppers, etc.), necessary for the formation of collagen, to increase immune defenses and along with other antioxidants found in these foods, to combat cell aging.

This group of foods also provides minerals such as potassium which regulates the saline balance of the cell, the rhythmicity of the heart and intervenes in the muscle contraction and transmission of the nervous impulse.

Recommended servings: 5 servings per day

Seasoning fats and oils:

Olive oil, seed oil or oilseed oil are preferred.

Fats and seasoning oils play an important role in providing

essential fatty acids and in promoting the absorption of fat-soluble vitamins (vitamins A, D, E, and K). The daily portions of this group of foods should be kept under control because excessive fat consumption can be harmful. A good habit is to always dose the oil in a spoon before pouring it on foods.

Recommended portions: 1-2 portions at lunch and dinner, considering each portion consisting of:
10 ml per oil (one soup spoon) or 10 grams butter

Milk and its derivatives:

This group includes not only milk but also yoghurt, dairy products, fresh and mature cheeses. These foods provide easily assimilable calcium, which is involved in the formation and maintenance of bone tissue and teeth and in the regulation of other important processes in the body, but also high-quality proteins and vitamins (such as B2 necessary for the release of energy into the cell and A). For breakfast, choose semi-skimmed milk or yoghurt (also good options for snacks) and add a spoonful of mature cheese to your first course and favor low-fat cheeses. Cheeses are an excellent second course, but they provide many calories; just think that one hectogram (100 grams) of mozzarella provides three times as many calories as cod. Compared to mozzarella, cow ricotta cheese has a lot less calories and is richer in calcium.

Recommended portions: 2 servings a day.

Nuts, seeds and flavorings:

nuts (walnuts, almonds, pine nuts, etc.) and seeds (sunflower, sesame, pumpkin, etc.) provide essential fatty acids (omega-3 and omega-6) and also provide fiber and vitamin E. Flavourings, such as herbs, spices, garlic and onions provide important protective substances.

Recommended portions: 1-2 servings per day of nuts or seeds, herbs and spices according to the recipe dishes.

FOODS TO INCLUDE IN YOUR DIET EVERY WEEK

Eggs, legumes, fish, white meat, red meat and cold cuts:

To ensure an ideal supply of excellent quality proteins you should alternate meat, a source of iron which can be easily assimilated, fish, a source of essential fats such as omega-3 and eggs, which are rich in phospholipids, in your diet. These foods also provide copper (necessary for the formation of red blood cells, pigmentation and maintenance of bone tissue), zinc (necessary for growth, healing and sensitivity of taste and smell), and vitamin B12 (necessary for the formation of red blood cells, nerve function and release of energy into the cell). This group also includes legumes, which in addition to protein and carbohydrates are a good source of fiber, minerals, vitamins, such as B3, useful for growth hormone formation and skin maintenance.

Recommended portions for eggs: Two to four servings a week.
Recommended portions for fish and legumes: Two or more servings per week.
Recommended portions for meat: One to three servings a week.

PROBIOTICS

Our intestines are colonized by a large number of microorganisms, partly beneficial and partly potentially harmful, which live in balance with each other and with the body. We now know that this large community of intestinal microorganisms can produce substances that are very beneficial to OUR health. For example, there are vitamins or molecules such as neurotransmitters, which can generate different feelings and emotions when they reach the brain. It is scientifically proven that the state of our intestines influences our mood and mental health, that's because the gut is connected to the brain through the vagus nerve.

Probiotics are "good" bacteria that come into play whenever the intestinal microflora is altered, for various reasons, and help to restore intestinal well-being.

Probiotics have an effect on many disorders, from digestive problems to anxiety and depression. Researchers in a 2011 study found that the administration of Lactobacillus Rhamnosus in mice increased GABA production and decreased stress, depression and anxiety-related behaviors. GABA is in fact a neurotransmitter that has an influence on mood.

It is believed that when you do not have enough GABA, you may end up suffering from anxiety, depression, epilepsy and chronic pain.

Interestingly, mice whose vagus nerve had been removed and received probiotics did not see the same results. This suggests that the improvement in resilience has something to do with the activation of the vagus nerve.

Some FERMENTED FOODS are naturally rich in probiotics, for example:

- <u>Yogurt and Fermented Milk</u>; yogurt is a food rich in probiotics par excellence because of the high amount of lactose that is fermented by probiotics. There are many strains of probiotics naturally present, or added, to yoghurt and they generally belong to the genus Lactobacillus and Bifidobacterium .

- <u>Kefir</u>, a drink based on fresh fermented milk typical of Russian culture. The milk can be FROM cow's, goat's or sheep's milk. Kefir usually contains good amounts of Lactobacilli and Saccaromycetes.

- <u>Miso and Tempeh</u>, typical foods of oriental cuisine derived from the fermentation of soy and other cereals such as barley, rice and buckwheat. In these foods, probiotic Lactobacilli colonies and good amounts of vitamin B12 are easily developed. Tempeh is also an excellent source of prebiotic fibres.

- <u>Sauerkraut</u>; widespread in Northern European countries (such as Austria and Germany), it is obtained by fermenting cabbage. In addition to several colonies of Lactobacilli contain high amounts of sodium, potassium and calcium. Sauerkraut are also good vitamin sources with a good content of vitamin B12 and vitamin C.

INTERMITTENT FASTING

Intermittent fasting can be beneficial to your health. It can enhance cognitive and mitochondrial function. It might likewise enhance the metabolic process and minimize the threat of cardiovascular disease and cancer. It turns out these health advantages are related to periodic fasting's capability to promote the vagus nerve and enhance vagal tone. A 2003 research study discovered that fasting is a physiological activator of the vagus nerve.

As the name suggests, intermittent fasting is a nutritional approach that alternates between periods of eating and periods of fasting. It isn't therefore a real diet, but a food program that more than suggesting what, tells you when to eat.

There are certain methods of intermittent fasting and the most popular are:

1- **Scheme 16/8**: Scheme 16/8: this scheme divides the day into two parts: 8 hours of eating and 16 hours of fasting. It can be considered as a prolongation of fasting which is done automatically when you sleep, skipping your breakfast and eating first meal at noon and then eating until 8.00 in the evening.

2- **Every other day (5:2)**: the idea of this model is that for 2 days a week you decrease your calorie intake to a maximum of 500/600 calories. The days do not have to be consecutive and on the other days you can eat what you want.

3- **Eat Stop Eat:** scheme in which you fast for 24 consecutive hours one or two days a week.

What to Eat and Drink in Intermittent Fasting? How Many Calories Should you Consume?

During fasting all foods that raise insulin levels should be excluded: not only carbohydrates, but also proteins and lipids. Water, calorie-free drinks (tea, coffee without sugar), micronutrient supplements are therefore allowed.

The calories to be consumed depend on what your weekly calorie needs are; once this is established, you can distribute the calories in the week according to the fasting protocol chosen.

In general, you can choose between:

- Fasting or reducing calories a lot on certain days of the week and eating normally on the remaining days;
- Insert fasting within the day (e.g. 16/8) and extend this pattern every day of the week.

What matters is that at the end of the week the set calorie balance returns.

The 16/8 method is the most widespread and also the one that can be most easily applied: it can be used for example by bringing dinner forward and skipping breakfast the next day.

A weekly scheme can include skipping dinner, so as to let the necessary time pass during the night, taking advantage of the sleep step. Thus the time window in which you can eat breakfast and lunch is reduced to 8 hours.

For example: breakfast at 7 a.m. and lunch by 3 p.m. Then only calorie-free liquids (i.e. no sugar, but preferably only water) until 7 a.m. the following morning. In this case sixteen hours would have passed. You can move this window from 8 am to 4 pm and resume the next morning at 8 am.

It is fundamental to maintain a certain regularity. Remembering that this diet, also called mima-feeding, must not be thwarted by eating too much and badly. The 16/8 method allows you to combine fasting for sixteen hours with exercise in the afternoon.

Benefits and Advantages of Intermittent Fasting

Fasting sets a new metabolic and hormonal balance and, when well calibrated, it is beneficial: it increases GH levels, energy expenditure, lipolysis and you can maintain good hunger control.

-Blood glucose
In response to hours without food, lower blood glucose levels are established, although clearly to avoid hypoglycemia a hormonal response is triggered to maintain adequate levels (such as decreased insulin and increased glucagon and catecholamines).

-Cortisol
Thanks to fasting, there is an increase in resistance to stress at the nervous, cardiac, muscular levels.

-Insulin
The positive effect is twofold: there is a decrease in insulin levels and at the same time an increase in insulin sensitivity, although not all subjects respond in the same way, and therefore it is advisable to evaluate this parameter after a couple of weeks.

-Immune system
As far as the immune system is concerned, there is a decrease in chronic systemic inflammation, i.e. in the whole body, but in particular in the nervous, adipose and gastro-intestinal tract.

-Sleep
Although fasting imposes a different hormone pattern than those who do not follow it, there are no repercussions with

regard to the quality of sleep, except when the feeding window is short and concentrated in the hours before going to sleep.

Questions and Answers Intermittent Fasting

Can you do intermittent fasting while training?
Yes, but you will need to evaluate your personal response to the effort: some people have better results if they train by fasting, others if they do so during the time window when they are consuming food. It depends on the person, the intensity of the training and the goal.

What are the differences between intermittent fasting and normal low-calorie diet?
In the low-calorie diet there is a non-periodic calorie restriction, which tends to be used in cases where the goal is only weight loss. Instead, intermittent fasting provides calorie restriction only on certain days or time slots, depending on the model adopted.

What are the differences between this and the ketogenic diet?
The ketogenic diet is a type of normocaloric protocol but with a distribution of nutrients that favors protein and fat at the expense of carbohydrates. Instead, intermittent fasting provides a balanced distribution of macronutrients but with a periodic calorie restriction.
The two protocols are united by the metabolic pathways that are activated with their practice, i.e. the production of ketones used for energy instead of carbohydrates.

What can you drink or eat during intermittent fasting?
You need to distinguish the time of fasting from the time when it is allowed to eat: in the former, any food that provides calories would make the effort futile, but it is possible to consume drinks without added sugar such as tea, herbal tea, water or coffee.

Any food may be eaten during the proper period, although nutritional value of the food and its general quality should be taken into consideration.

Is it good to take supplements when fasting?
Some types of supplements are necessary during a normal diet, so it is good to continue their intake even during a period of intermittent fasting, where the risk of micro deficiencies is higher.

Can intermittent fasting be practiced at any time of life?
In some physiological periods the practice of intermittent fasting is not recommended, as in the case of pregnancy, breastfeeding, childhood and development. It is not appropriate when attempting to conceive.

Better to skip breakfast, lunch or dinner?
In the 16/8 scheme, you can decide which meals can be avoided, but skipping breakfast or dinner is easier to manage.

SOUND AND THE VAGUS NERVE

There are many noted ways to stimulate the vagus nerve and they include: singing, laughing, yoga, meditation, breathing exercises, movement in general and sound. Singing and laughing train the muscles in the throat, which activates the nerve. Regulated yoga practice, meditation and OM-chanting can also increase the activation of this nerve. All of these ways of stimulating the vagus nerve have one thing in common: sound.

Doctors believe the resonance frequency of organs can restore the body to a healthy state and it can help with diseases such as anxiety, PTSD, migraines, depression and memory disorders, chronic pain, sleep disorders and even cancer. Scholars from the University of Toronto, Wilfrid Laurier University and Baycrest Center hospitals conducted a study of patients at various stages of disease by subjecting them to a 40-Hertz sound simulation. They found "hopeful" results with cognition, clarity and alertness. Some authors of these facts said that "certain parts of the brain appear to be on the same communication frequency, and this frequency is around 40 Hz.

If you have too little, the two sections of the brain that want to talk to one another, like the short-term memory and the long-term memory, will not communicate, so they will not have long-term memory. "Bartel explained that the noise simulation processing at 40 Hz leads to an "increased" frequency with which "parts of the brain can speak again".

A certain mindset comes from a French ENT doctor, Alfred A. Tomatis, who believes that the main function of the ear is to provide electrical stimulation to all body cells, "which strengthens the whole and gives people more dynamism" (Tomatis. 1978). He believes that the abundant sounds in the high harmonics are considered charge sounds, and the abundant sounds in the bass sounds are considered discharge sounds. Tomatis claimed to have successfully treated a variety of sound disorders as they are all related to inner ear problems. Some of the problems that he successfully treated were stuttering, depression, ADD, difficulty concentrating, and balance problems.

Another study suggests that the Tomatis method is helpful in supporting children with ADD. The results showed statistically significant improvements for Tomatis compared to the non-Tomatis group. The experimental group showed significant improvements in processing speed, phonological awareness and efficiency of phonemic decoding during reading, behavior and attention to hearing.

Sound is becoming one of the most widely used methods of alternative healing. It is a brilliant method of everyday healing to stimulate the vagus nerve, by promoting the health and vitality of all organs in your body. This is thanks to sound healing and singing bowls made of chakra crystal.

Clear Quartz is called a "master healer" because it has the ability to amplify, transform, and transmit energy. When working with these quartz glass bowls, the effects on organs, tissues and cells as well as on the circulatory, hormone and metabolic system are significant. The tones of the crystals are perceived by the ear, felt in the body, and they stimulate the vagus nerve and vibrate through every chakra center in the body, creating a balanced and rejuvenated mind, body and spirit.

VAGUS NERVE IN THE MEDIA

Medical interventions that can cure many physical and mental health problems have been discussed in several articles (wired.com; businessinsider.com, huffingtonpost.com).

The focus is on the vagus nerve as a potential "switch" for inflammation-related diseases such as epilepsy, rheumatoid arthritis and inflammatory bowel syndrome. Vagus nerve regulation also plays an important role in mental health care so you can respond efficiently to the emotional and physiological signs of depression, PTSD, and anxiety.

The field of bioelectronic medicine offers vagus nerve stimulation (VNS) as an intervention to treat rheumatoid arthritis, epilepsy and depression through the surgical implantation of tiny electronic devices that can cause shocks to the vagus nerve. Other research is concerned with non-invasive external devices that stimulate the vagus nerve through the skin. The long-term effects of these "electroceutical products" can be promising for people with chronic illnesses, depression and PTSD.

The vagus nerve is important for controlling your immune system. There is a close relationship between chronic stress, immune function and inflammation. In short, the short-term activation of your sympathetic nervous system releases cortisols and helps keep your immune system at a healthy level. Long-term stress, on the other hand, suppresses immunity. Chronic traumatic stress leaves your immune system uncontrolled and leads to inflammation in the body.

Activating the vagus nerve keeps your immune system at bay and releases a number of hormones and enzymes such as acetylcholine and oxytocin. This leads to a reduction in inflammation, an improvement in memory and a feeling of relaxation. Vagus nerve stimulation can decrease allergic reactions and tension headaches.

INFLAMMATION OF THE BRAIN

RELATIONSHIP BETWEEN INTESTINAL INFLAMMATION AND BRAIN INFLAMMATION

The relationship between inflammation of the intestine and inflammation of the brain can impact your health significantly. Current science strongly supports the idea that the inflammatory process actually begins in the gastrointestinal tract, which then spreads and affects the brain.

What are the triggers of intestinal inflammation? To the surprise of many, it's mostly food:

• Eating too many carbohydrates leads to high chronic blood sugar. The increase in blood sugar increases the binding of glucose to proteins. This process, known as glycation, significantly increases the level of inflammation in the body.

• Opting for a low-fat diet, eating too few healthy fats or eating the wrong types of processed and rancid fats.

• Insufficient intake of antioxidants, which are mainly found in fruits, vegetables and herbs.

• Eating too much food that is loaded with irritants and toxins such as chemicals, preservatives, pesticides, GMOs and heavy metals.

• Having an undiagnosed sensitivity to gluten.

• The overgrowth of Candida yeasts, the overgrowth of small intestine bacteria (SIBO) and intestinal parasites trigger the immune response and lead to intestinal inflammation.

HOW TO PREVENT INFLAMMATION OF THE BRAIN

Inflammation is a natural defense of our body against something that it believes is potentially dangerous. For example, should you twist your ankle, your body will suffer from stress. The natural response is to cause swelling and pain to reduce movement and promote healing. These are the characteristics of the inflammatory process; in small doses it's not a negative thing. It only gets bad if the inflammation becomes uncontrollable and chronic. Chronic inflammation is usually mild, quiet, and has no symptoms. If the body is under constant attack, the inflammatory reaction remains active and spreads to all parts of the body via the bloodstream. The brain is extremely sensitive because it is also connected to the intestine via the vagus nerve.

Uncontrolled inflammation leads to the production of a variety of inflammatory chemicals called cytokines that are toxic to cells. Cytokines move throughout the body and cause oxidative stress, which leads to decreased cell function and even cell destruction, and actual loss of function in the body. Studies using new imaging technologies have shown a dramatic increase in inflammatory cytokines in the brain of Alzheimer's patients and people with other brain disorders. So, to prevent inflammation of the brain, the most important thing is to maintain a healthy gut.

Food That Nourishes the Gut and Brain

The reason why inflammation is so common in western civilization is modern nutrition. It is rich in flammable foods such as refined flour, excessive sugar, oxidized or rancid fats, trans fats, and a variety of chemicals and preservatives. And it contains little anti-inflammatory foods like long chain omega-

3 fatty acids, fermented foods and fermentable fiber.

There is a large number of foods that are especially good for the gut and brain:

- Beets
- Blueberries
- Bone broth (to heal the inflammatory intestinal mucosa)
- Broccoli
- Coconut oil (used as an alternative fuel for our brain, except glucose)
- Celery
- Dark chocolate
- Egg yolk
- Fermented foods (rich in bacteria that keep the intestines healthy, e.g. kimchee, sauerkraut, pickled vegetables, yogurt and fermented drinks such as kombucha and kefir)
- Fermentable fiber (as food for good intestinal bacteria such as asparagus, artichokes, garlic, jicama leek and onions)
- Extra virgin olive oil
- Green, leafy vegetables
- Rosemary (anti-inflammatory)
- Alaskan salmon, caught in the wild
- Sardines
- Turmeric (anti-inflammatory)

Exercise to Reduce Inflammation

Exercises tend to favor acute inflammation, but if they are carried out regularly, in the long term they reduce chronic inflammation. The oxidative stress of training forces your body to develop your antioxidant defenses. This has been proven in studies showing that extended exercise programs reduce inflammation markers, like insulin resistance and highly sensitive C-reactive protein (an indicator of diabetes).

However, some people tend to exercise too much, and it is extremely important to allow adequate recovery, especially when training at high intensity intervals (repeated sprints interspersed with recovery). If you exercise too much, like a marathon, it can do more harm than good, as your body has to be restored from the damage (acute inflammation) suffered during training.

An average American adult spends about 10 hours a day sitting. Research shows that this degree of inactivity cannot even be compensated for with a 60-minute workout at the end of each day. So what should you do when you have a corporate job? Understand that the body needs almost continuous movement throughout the day. You should stand up from your chair and go for a walk at least every 50 minutes.

One way to increase activity is to just walk more. It is recommended to aim for 7,000 to 10,000 steps a day. A fitness tracker is an important tool to help you achieve your daily goal.

Lack of Sleep Affects Brain Function

Deprivation of sleep is really bad for brain function. Many studies show that sleep deprivation affects various cognitive functions and behaviors, including arousal, attention, cognitive speed, memory, emotional intelligence, and decision making.

Utilizing imaging techniques like functional magnetic resonance imaging (fMRI), scientists compared the brain of a person with a lack of sleep to the brain of a person who slept normally. They found a decrease in metabolism and blood flow in several regions of the brain, which indicated an impairment of cognitive functions and behavior.

Several nights of poor sleep or a sleepless night will upset your hormonal balance. According to the research in Stanford

University, your body's ghrelin levels, which cause hunger attacks, can increase by almost 15%. It also lowers your leptin level, a hormone that regulates energy levels. This is why you seem to feel lazy when you miss sleep.

Your brain also has problems organizing and sorting new memories. You can pick up new information, but your brain has trouble accessing and using it. You may feel distracted as your response time decreases. This makes responsibilities like driving more challenging and dangerous.

A CDC feedback shows that half of Americans (48%) do not get sufficient rest. So if you want your brain to stay in shape, you need to put sleep at the top of your priority list. In the event that you simply cannot sleep enough, a 30-minute nap is still helpful, even if the negative consequences of sleep deprivation cannot be completely eliminated.

Vitamin D Can Save Your Brain

Much has been learned about the health benefits of vitamin D in the past decade. Although it has long been known that vitamin D supports strong, healthy bones, its role in diseases of the brain is becoming increasingly clear.

A new study that has involved several respected institutions around the world has found a deep correlation between low vitamin D levels and an increased risk of dementia. Even a moderate vitamin D deficiency was associated with a 53% increased risk of dementia. Severely disabled people had an increased risk of 122%!

Many people do not know that vitamin D deficiency is associated with increased inflammation. There are around 30,000 genes in the body and almost 3,000 of them are affected by vitamin D. Your brain also has vitamin D receptors. So if you're not exposed to the sun for 20 minutes a day (without sunscreen on your face, arms, and legs), you may want to think of taking a supplement.

Most people need about 5,000 IU a day to reach the optimal value of 50 to 70 ng / ml determined by a blood test. If you supplement, choose vitamin D3, which is the natural form, and take it with vitamin K2 with at least 100 µg of menaquinone-7 (MK-7). The combination of D3 and K2 causes calcium to be deposited in the bones instead of the arteries.

Think positive and stimulate your brain.

Stress and fear kill existing brain neurons and prevent new neurons from forming. Research has shown that positive thinking accelerates cell formation and significantly reduces stress and anxiety. So catch yourself when your negative thoughts come up, throw them away and replace them with positive thoughts.

As you learn or do new things, new neural pathways are developed. That is why you want to continuously stimulate your brain. Do you remember the phrase 'use it or lose it'?

STIMULATION OF THE VAGUS NERVE AS A MEDICAL TREATMENT

More and more studies suggest that we can manipulate or "hack" the vagus nerve. The vagus hacks date back to some studies by Kevin Tracey in 1998. Through his work, he discovered that stimulating the vagus nerve with an electrical impulse reduced the body's inflammatory response.

Vagus nerve stimulation is a medical cure that tries to treat a variety of diseases. This can be done manually or by electrical impulses. Based on the efficiency of vagus nerve stimulation in clinical studies, the United States Food and Drug Administration (FDA) gave the approval to its use in the treatment of two different diseases; epilepsy and mental illness.

HOW IT IS DONE

A little electrical device, similar to a pacemaker, is placed in a person's chest, by placing a lead around the right branch of the vagus nerve and implanting a battery under the clavicle. This device is put into the body through surgery under general anesthesia. Electrical impulses are then sent to the brain at regular intervals via the vagus nerve.

According to the Mayo Clinic, Europe has approved a vagus nerve stimulator that does not require surgical implantation.

VNS and Epilepsy

In 1997, the FDA endorsed the use of vagus nerve stimulation in refractory epilepsy. The implanted device regularly stimulates the nerve which, according to the Epilepsy

Foundation, reduces or even prevents excessive brain activity that leads to seizures.

Vagus nerve stimulation in epilepsy can have some side effects:

- Hoarseness or voice changes
- Sore throat
- Breathlessness
- Coughing
- Slow heart rate
- Difficulty swallowing
- Stomach discomfort or nausea

People using this type of treatment should always tell their doctor if they have any problems, as there are ways to reduce or stop them.

VNS and Mental Illness

Research has revealed that vagus nerve stimulation can be effective in treating psychiatric disorders that do not respond to medication. A study published in a 2008 journal, Brain Stimulation, found that stimulation of the vagus nerve leads to an improvement in symptoms in patients with treatment-resistant anxiety disorders such as obsessive-compulsive disorder, panic disorders and post-traumatic stress disorder.

In 2005, the FDA endorsed the use of vagus nerve stimulation to treat depression. It has also been seen to help the following conditions:

- Rapid cycle bipolar disorder
- Anxiety disorders
- Alzheimer's disease

VNS and Chronic Illness

Since the vagus nerve reaches almost all organs in the body, researchers are trying to find out whether stimulations can help with other diseases. Researchers have observed the role of the vagus nerve in the treatment of chronic inflammatory diseases such as sepsis, lung damage, rheumatoid arthritis (RA) and diabetes.

Since the vagus nerve affects the immune system, nerve damage can play a role in autoimmune diseases and other diseases. These conditions include:
- Rheumatoid arthritis
- Cardiac arrest
- Diabetes mellitus
- Persistent hiccups
- Abnormal heart rhythm
- Inflammation of Crohn's disease

In the case of rheumatoid arthritis, which disturbs 1.3 million adults in the United States, a 2016 study in the Proceedings of the National Academy of Sciences (PNAS), showed that stimulating the vagus nerve can help alleviate symptoms and "significantly improved the measurement of disease activity in patients with rheumatoid arthritis". People who did not respond to any other treatment reported significant improvements, and no serious side effects were found.

The birth of implants to stimulate the vagus nerve using electronic implants has shown a drastic reduction and even remission of rheumatoid arthritis, which is incurable and is often treated with toxic drugs.

There was a real breakthrough when it was found that vagus nerve stimulation could treat not only rheumatoid arthritis, but also other inflammatory diseases such as Crohn's disease, Parkinson's disease and Alzheimer's disease. New research has shown that this nerve could also be the missing link in the treatment of chronic inflammation, and the start of an exciting new treatment area for serious and incurable diseases.

With the success of stimulating the vagus nerve to treat inflammation and epilepsy, a burgeoning area of medical research, known as bioelectronics, could be the future of medicine. By using implants that provide electrical impulses to different parts of the body, scientists and doctors hope to treat diseases with fewer drugs and fewer side effects.

VNS Procedures

There is no physical participation of the brain in this operation, and patients generally cannot feel the impulses. It is important to note that VNS is a treatment option that is limited to certain people with therapy-resistant epilepsy or depression.

People with one of the following criteria may be unsuitable candidates for VNS:
- People who use other accompanying forms of brain stimulation
- Irregular heartbeat or other heart defects
- Dysautonomia (functional disorders of the autonomic nervous system)
- Diseases or disorders of the lungs (shortness of breath, asthma, etc.)
- Ulcers (stomach, duodenum, etc.)
- Vasovagal syncope (fainting)
- Pre-existing hoarseness

VNS Implementation

This procedure is performed by a neurosurgeon and usually lasts about 45 to 90 minutes, with the patient most often being under general anesthesia. It is performed on an outpatient basis. As with all operations, the risk of infection is low. Other surgical drawbacks of VNS include inflammation or pain at the incision site, damage to nearby nerves, and nerve narrowing.

The process requires two small cuts. The first is on the upper left side of the chest, where the pulse generator is located. A second cut is made horizontally along the fold of the skin on the left side of the lower neck. This is where the thin, flexible wires are inserted that connect the pulse generator to the vagus nerve.

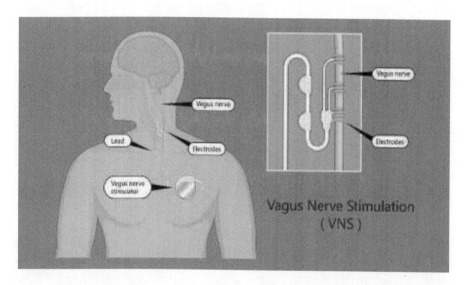

Vagus Nerve Stimulation (VNS)

The device or fixture is a flat, round piece of metal with a diameter of approximately 4 cm and a thickness of 10-13 mm, depending on the model used. The stimulator contains a battery that, if it runs low, the pacemaker is replaced with a less invasive procedure that only requires opening the incision in the chest wall.

The pacemaker is most often activated two to four weeks after implantation, although in some cases it can be activated in the operating room at the time of surgery. The treating neurologist wires the stimulator in his office with a small handheld computer, programming software and a programming stick. The strength and length of the electrical impulses are programmed. The level of stimulation varies from case to case, but is usually initiated at a low level and slowly increased to a level appropriate for the individual. The device works continuously and is programmed in such a way that it switches on and off for certain periods, e.g. 30 seconds when switching on and 5 minutes when switching off.

Patients receive a portable magnet to control the pacemaker at home. If the magnet is passed over the pulse generator point, an additional stimulation is given regardless of the treatment program. If you hold the magnet over the pulse generator, stimulation is deactivated when the magnet is in position. If you remove it, the stimulation cycle will continue.

The side effects are mostly related to stimulation and usually improve over time. They can include:

- Hoarseness
- Increased cough
- Changes in voice / language
- General pain
- Sore throat or neck pain
- Cramps in the throat or larynx
- Headache
- Insomnia
- Indigestion
- Muscle movements or contractions related to stimulation
- Nausea or vomiting
- Changed sense of touch
- Tingling of the skin

Among these, hoarseness, coughing, tingling in the throat and shortness of breath are the most common and usually temporary.

Advice / Guidelines for Patients

If you have received a VNS, you should monitor your condition and general health consistently. If any of the following happen, call your doctor immediately:

- Constantly hoarse voice
- Stimulation that becomes painful or irregular
- Stimulation that causes choking, breathing or swallowing, or a change in heart rate
- Changes in your level of awareness, such as increased drowsiness
- Indications that the pulse generator is not stimulated correctly or the battery is empty (the device has stopped working)
- Any new or unusual changes specifically related to stimulation

You should also call your doctor before undergoing medical tests that can affect the VNS, such as Magnetic Resonance Imaging (MRI) or before you implant another medical device.

VNS can be seen as a treatment option in patients who have tried at least two antiepileptic drugs (AEDs) without adequate seizure control, or in patients who have not responded to AEDs and who cannot undergo brain surgery. It is important to note that VNS is used in conjunction with AEDs and not instead of them. In addition, VNS is seen as a palliative process that can effectively improve crisis management, but generally does not create complete freedom from confiscation. VNS can take up to two years to treat a patient's seizures. If the VNS is effective, it can allow a patient to decrease the DEA doses over a period of time.

The goal of VNS is to decrease the number, duration and severity of seizures. VNS can also shorten the time it takes to recover from a crisis. However, VNS does not work in all patients. The success of this treatment varies - some patients report less frequent seizures, others a little reduction, while some victims do not respond at all.

The following results have been seen in some epilepsy patients:
- Less severe or shorter crises

- Better recovery from seizures (postictal phase)
- Improved well-being
- Better mood
- Improved attention, memory and cognitive skills
- Fewer emergency room visits
- For people with warnings before their seizures, activating the pacemaker with the magnet can help to shorten or even stop the seizures when the warning occurs.

Shortly after VNS was approved by the FDA as a crisis treatment, reports indicated a possible decrease in symptoms of depression in patients who had the seizure control device implanted. As with electro-seizure therapy, it is believed that VNS uses electricity to influence the production of brain chemicals called neurotransmitters. Depression is linked to an imbalance in these chemicals.

In studies of more than 200 patients with treatment-resistant depression (TRD), the device showed no benefit in the first two or three months. However, after one year, 20-30% of the patients reported significant improvements, and half of these patients reported that their symptoms had almost completely disappeared. However, other patients didn't improve, or their symptoms worsened.

VNS should not be considered for patients with any of the following symptoms:
- Acute thoughts or behavior of suicide
- History of schizophrenia, schizoaffective disorder, or delusional disease
- History of fast cycle bipolar disorder

There is much debating about the efficacy of VNS in treating TRD, and more data on the results are in the works.

The new non-invasive vagus nerve stimulation device has been approved in Europe for the treatment of epilepsy, depression and pain; these do not require surgical implantation. A non-invasive device that stimulates the vagus nerve has recently been approved by the Food and Drug Administration for the cure of cluster headaches in the United States.

About a third of epileptics do not respond fully to antiepileptics. Vagus nerve stimulation can be an option to reduce the frequency of seizures in people who have failed to control medication. Vagus nerve stimulation can also be useful for people who have not responded to intensive treatments for depression, such as antidepressants, psychological counseling (psychotherapy), and electro-seizure therapy (ECT).

The Food and Drug Administration (FDA) supported vagus nerve stimulation for people who:
- Are over 4 years of age
- Have focal (partial) epilepsy
- Have seizures that aren't well controlled with medication

The FDA has also allowed vagus nerve stimulation to treat depression in adults that:
- Have chronic depression that is difficult to treat (treatment-resistant depression)
- Have not improved after trying at least four types of medication or electro-cramp therapy (ECT) or both
- Have continuous standard treatments for depression and vagus nerve stimulation

In addition, researchers are investigating vagus nerve stimulation as a possible treatment for a variety of diseases, including headaches, rheumatoid arthritis, inflammatory bowel diseases, bipolar disorders, obesity and dementia.

Make an Appointment

For most people, stimulation of the vagus nerve is safe. However, there are certain risks during the implantation operation of the device and brain stimulation.

Surgery Risks

Surgical complications, from the stimulation of the implanted vagus nerve, are rare and comparable to the dangers of other surgical procedures. They include:
- Pain where the incision is made to implant the device
- Infection
- Difficulties swallowing
- Vocal cord paralysis, which is usually short-term, but can be permanent

Side Effects After Surgery

Some of the side effects and health issues related to stimulating the implanted vagus nerve may include:
- Voice changes
- Hoarseness
- Sore throat
- Cough
- Headache
- Breathlessness
- Difficulties swallowing
- Tingling of the skin
- Insomnia
- Worsening of sleep apnoea

The side effects are tolerable for most people. Some side effects can remain bothersome for the duration of vagus nerve treatment. These effects can be minimized by adapting the electrical pulses. If the side effects are unbearable, the device can be switched off temporarily or permanently.

How to Prepare

It is important to deliberately weigh the pros and cons of stimulating the implanted vagus nerve before deciding on the procedure. Make sure you know all the other treatment options and that you and your doctor both think that implanted vagus nerve stimulation is the best option for you. Ask your doctor specifically what you can expect during the operation and after switching on the pulse generator.

Food and Medicine

You may need to avoid certain medicines in advance, and your doctor may ask you to stop eating the night before the procedure.

What Can You Expect?

Before the procedure:

Your doctor will conduct a physical exam before the surgery. You may need to have a blood sample taken to make sure you don't have any health issues that could be an issue. Your doctor can request that you take antibiotics before surgery to prevent infection.

During the procedure:

Surgery to implant the vagus nerve stimulator can be done on an outpatient basis, although some surgeons recommend staying overnight.

The surgery normally takes one to one and a half hours. You can stay awake but take medication to numb the operating area (local anesthesia) or may be operated on while unconscious (general anesthesia). The surgery itself doesn't affect your brain. Two incisions are made, one on the chest or in the armpit area, and the other on the left part of the neck. The pulse generator is in the upper left corner of your chest. The device is intended to be a permanent implant but can be removed if necessary.

The pulse generator is the size of a stopwatch and is operated by a battery. A supply cable is connected to the pulse generator. The guidewire is passed under the skin from the chest to the neck, where it is attached to the left vagus nerve via the second incision.

After the procedure:

The pulse generator is switched on during a visit to your doctor's office a few weeks after the operation. Then it can be rewired to deliver electrical impulses to the vagus nerve at different times, frequencies and currents. Vagus nerve stimulation usually begins at a low level and gradually increases depending on your symptoms and side effects.

The stimulation is programmed to turn on and off in certain cycles. When nerve stimulation is activated, tingling or slight neck pain and temporary hoarseness can occur.

The pacemaker does not recognize seizure activity or symptoms of depression. When switched on, the pacemaker switches on and off at the intervals specified by your doctor. You can use a portable magnet to start stimulation at a different time, for example, when an attack is imminent.

The magnet can also be used to disable vagus nerve stimulation for a short while. This may be necessary when you are doing certain activities, for example, speaking, singing, exercising in public, or eating when you have trouble swallowing. You need to see your doctor regularly to make sure that the pulse generator is working properly and has not moved. Consult your doctor before taking medical tests such as magnetic resonance imaging (MRI) that could interfere with your device.

Results

Implanted vagus nerve stimulation is not a cure for epilepsy. Most people with epilepsy will not stop having seizures or taking epilepsy medication after the procedure. But many will have fewer seizures, up to 20 to 50% less. The intensity of the seizures can also decrease.

It can take months or even more than a year for you to notice a significant decrease in seizures. Vagus nerve stimulation can also decrease recovery time after an attack. People who have received vagus nerve stimulation to treat epilepsy, may also notice an improvement in mood and quality of life.

The benefits of implanted vagus nerve stimulation in the

treatment of depression are still inconsistent. Some studies suggest that the benefits increase over time, and it may take at least a few months for you to notice improvement in your depression symptoms. The implanted vagus nerve stimulation does not work for everyone and is not intended to replace conventional treatments.

The studies on stimulating the vagus nerve that was implanted to treat diseases like Alzheimer's, headache, and rheumatoid arthritis were too small to make clear conclusions about how they could work for these problems.

COMMERCIAL VNS DEVICES

How do commercial VNS devices differ from conventional clinical devices?

In addition to the differences in frequencies and voltages, a fully external VNS device obviously cannot be implanted directly on the nerve, as is the case with clinical devices. Commercial VNS devices rely on electrical signals that can penetrate the skin and neck muscles, without affecting the permeable tissue. It still has to be precise enough to access and regulate the specific activity of the nerve.

Clinical VNS devices avoid stimulation of the small fibers of the vagus nerve that cause pain and which should be avoided. However, the larger fibers entering the brain are more likely to be the target for possible treatments. Targeting these fibers is hard for an external device that cannot be bound to certain nerve fibers.

Some VNS devices available on the market are medical devices that need the approval of a doctor. Others claim to be entertainment devices for reducing stress . How do you use these devices and what are the risks?

Because of this strong connection to the heart, commercial VNS devices have serious potential side effects, such as cardiac arrest. Improper stimulation can cause problems with the heart system and trigger a heart attack. For this reason, VNS devices are generally only used on the right side of the nerve because they have a less direct connection to the heart.

We do not yet know the long-term effects of this treatment. If you overstimulate the nerves, they can release neurotransmitters that cause inflammation, both at the treatment site and further down in the circuits. In older people, these nerves are more likely to be damaged by inflammation. While treating central nervous system symptoms, you can damage the peripheral nervous system. As with many medical interventions, there is a balance between the benefits and drawbacks of the treatment and whether they can be tolerated.

Any patient seeking VNS treatment should speak to a doctor who specializes in this area. These devices can usually only be available on prescription. A doctor who is familiar with clinical studies and technologies has the relevant expertise. These devices are being introduced into the clinical environment faster than drugs. Non-invasive devices are obviously new, but when used in a clinical setting, they can reduce the risk of potential complications during surgery.

VNS devices could signal a big change in how these different conditions can be dealt with. All common drugs have side effects. If such a device can improve your life and how you work, finding out more and speaking to a doctor may be worthwhile.

INFLAMMATION AND THE VAGUS NERVE

WHAT IS INFLAMMATION?

Nature has equipped us with natural defense mechanisms that safeguard us from harmful external threats and internal stresses such as infections. The internal defense mechanisms are facilitated by the nervous system and the immune system. We are susceptible to different kinds of attacks; pneumonia, flu, sore throats, and bronchitis are all common ailments that result from pathogenic infections.

The immune system functions by identifying pathogens in the body and eliminating them. This means that our ability to fight off and recover from infections is dependent on the capacity of the immune system to identify and eliminate the disease-causing pathogen.

One of the methods that the immune system uses to identify and fight infection by pathogens and heal itself is inflammation.

An inflammatory response is triggered by the immune system to aid in the healing of wounds or infections from pathogens or tissue damage. Inflammatory reactions such as swelling when you hurt yourself or redness of a wound or secretion of pus are a sign that the body is fighting the infection by mobilizing white blood cells to the site of infection. Without inflammation, healing of wounds, infections, and tissue damage would be impossible.

Inflammation can either be acute or chronic, depending on what caused it and how long it lasts.

ACUTE AND CHRONIC INFLAMMATION

Acute inflammation is short-term inflammation and may be caused for example by tonsillitis, physical damage such as cuts and scrapes on the skin, bronchitis, or a sore throat. Typically, these conditions will last for a few days or a week, so the inflammation is not prolonged.

Chronic inflammation, on the other hand, occurs when inflammation is protracted and lasts for a long renga of time (from weeks to months or years). Some of the cases that are characterized by chronic inflammation include:

• Asthma
• Rheumatoid arthritis
• Crohn's disease
• Periodontitis
• Tuberculosis
• Chronic peptic ulcers

Chronic inflammation can result from an overactive immune system response to an infection, pathogens, or foreign antigen remaining in the body for extended periods or from pathogens that the body cannot break down. When an immune response is protracted, it starts to cause self-harm to the body by targeting healthy cells in much the same way it would invading pathogens.

HOW TO REDUCE CHRONIC INFLAMMATION

The vagus nerve, with its parasympathetic roles in the nervous system, helps inhibit the effects of overactive immune responses such as chronic inflammation by detecting the presence of cytokines and the tumor necrosis factor that is produced by the immune system. Once these compounds are detected, the vagus nerve signals the brain, and this signal initiates the production of anti-inflammatory neurotransmitters such as acetylcholine.

The vagus nerve also acts through the splenic nerve to curb the release of the tumor necrosis factor by macrophages, and in this way, functions to reduce and inhibit inflammation in the body.

If the immune system is not inhibited effectively by the parasympathetic nervous system, chronic inflammation can cause disorders in tissues and organs and ultimately impact the physical and psychological health of the individual.

Another benefit to having a toned vagus nerve is the reduction in inflammation throughout the body. Studies have shown when the vagus nerve is activated regularly and repeatedly, the usual response is inflammation will lessen. You will be able to better cope with this because the vagus nerve is the part of the body responsible for the ways in which you are able to defeat the inflammation cycle.

When you are suffering from inflammation, you can run into many health problems. You could also suffer from anxiety, depression, autoimmune disorders.

Studies have shown that, by activating the vagus nerve regularly and repeatedly, there are improvements in people suffering from Alzheimer's disease or rheumatoid arthritis.

The results are obvious—when you lower inflammation, a lot of the body actually becomes healthier than it had been in a very long time, and all you had to do was ensure you were better taking care of the way you approached your life.

Inflammation is a sign of harm to the body and may be caused by any number of things, ranging from poor nutrition to predisposed genetic conditions. And while you've probably heard of supplements like turmeric and even expensive detox programs to repair damaged cells, responding to inflammation may be a little easier than you might think. Simple exercise training can be one of the best solutions to reduce and even prevent it.

1. Exercise Regularly

Regular exercise is the right key to a healthy life plan. Despite the pain and stiffness you are feeling, exercising is important. Regular movements maintain flexibility and reduce stiffness and pain. Even a few minutes at a time can help. Your doctor, physiotherapist, or occupational therapist may recommend specific exercises depending on the severity of your symptoms. When looking for home workouts, focus on low impact workouts, such as walking and swimming.

Water exercises allow more freedom of movement in your joints, without the effect of a weight load. If done in warm water, it can also increase blood circulation. This can help reduce inflammation. Also consider exercises that improve mobility, such as tai chi and yoga. Regular exercise can be important if your doctor tells you to lose weight to improve your condition.

2. Adopt an Anti-Inflammatory Diet

Many experts recommend an anti-inflammatory or a Mediterranean diet for general health. Anti-inflammatory diets not only reduce inflammation in the body, but also the risk of heart disease. When it comes to inflammation, you will find that anti-inflammatory foods can improve your symptoms in the long run.

An anti-inflammatory diet mainly consists of plant foods such as fruits and vegetables, and moderate amounts of cereals and lentils. This type of diet also emphasizes seafood, but less dairy and meat. Mediterranean diets also include a lot of olive oil, which is good for your heart.

If you are considering a strong change in your diet to relieve your symptoms, you should also avoid flammable foods. These include sugar, trans fats, red meat, processed foods and fast food products.

3. Make Sleep a Priority

Sleep is another important part of health. Inflammation can occur in a body deprived of sleep, which aggravates pain, stiffness and fatigue. In addition, lack of sleep can lead to less exercise, more stress, and poor food choices.

Studies recommend that adults sleep at least seven hours a night. If you're over 60, you may need seven to nine hours a night. If your current sleep rate is below this value, you should go to bed a little earlier than you usually do each night until you reach your goal.

Inflammation can make you tired in the middle of the day, especially if you feel stiff and painful. Avoid napping during the day as this can disrupt your sleep schedule at night.

4. Stop Drinking and Smoking

Alcohol consumption and smoking are not recommended for people with inflammation, as they can lead to further problems. If your condition changes, you can develop weaker ribs that can affect your breathing. If you smoke more, your breathing difficulties may be worse. Talk to your doctor about various ways to quit drinking and smoking.

5. Find Ways to Reduce Stress

Stress does not discriminate. If you have inflammation, stressors related to work, childcare, school, and other commitments can make your symptoms worse. Stress can increase inflammation. Research shows that persistent stress and inflammation can lead to chronic illnesses later in life. Because inflammation is a precursor to other problems, it is all the more important to remove stress in your life.

While you can't ignore all of your obligations and responsibilities, there are ways you can relieve stress on a daily basis.

Here are some natural ways to alleviate stress:

- Meditate for 5-10 minutes each day.
- Start doing yoga.
- Go for a walk outside.
- Spend time in nature.
- Read a book.
- Take a warm bubble bath.
- Delegate tasks to family and friends.

6. Keeping Track

Tracking your treatment plan is one of the best forms of personal care. Make sure you don't miss any of your scheduled appointments, take your medication as directed, and follow your doctor as recommended. You should inform your doctor if your symptoms worsen or do not improve with treatment.

Just in time for the busiest season, MindBodyGreen has brought in experts to share specific anti-inflammatory exercises so you can stay healthy for the coming year. And you don't need a strenuous fitness program to get results. Studies highlight the importance of adopting exercise as an anti-inflammatory, citing "4,000 middle-aged people over a 10-year period have found that those who exercise for 2.5 hours a week reduced their inflammation by 12%."

1. **Foam Roll**. The foam roller rejuvenates the body by improving flexibility, strengthening the core and promoting digestion and blood flow. It may also be used to target

inflammation, as explained by Nicholas M. Licameli, physiotherapist at Professional Physiotherapy. He instructs his clients to "lie on a roller and use gravity to exert pressure on a muscle. The roller is pushed into the muscles of the belly and the user rolls the length of the target muscle up and down."

2. Deep Breathing and Yoga. Yoga and breathing exercises are effective methods of preventing inflammation, as Licameli provides the simple explanation that "deep, controlled breathing and meditation cause a state of relaxation. This is incredibly helpful if you have inflammation that you want to reduce in the body."

3. Walking. Walking is a useful strategy for anyone who is unable to participate in an intense fitness program, like Michelle Cady, health trainer and founder of FitVista, explains: "Walking is a great way to help your muscles recover; inflammation is reduced by sending fresh blood and oxygen through your body, pumping the lymphatic system to get rid of waste, and gently restoring your digestive system when it feels uncomfortable. "

Treatment of inflammation includes medication and therapies that prevent your condition from worsening over time.

ANXIETY AND THE VAGUS NERVE

DEFINING ANXIETY

Anxiety is another aspect that becomes incredibly relevant to the vagus nerve, as we have reiterated several times now. The way your body responds to anxiety is typically the same every time —you find that your heart races, you feel like you are in danger, and you begin to panic. This is a very normal feeling, and in moderation, there is nothing wrong with anxiety at all.

Anxiety is considered a disorder when it becomes detrimental to your life; when it begins to have that constant negative effect on you, it may be time to entertain whether or not you may have an anxiety problem. It is a disorder that can lead to feelings of nervousness, fear, worry, and apprehension to an excessive level.

When this happens, it may have a major impact on the way in which you respond to the world. It can change the way that you see what is happening around you. It can influence the way in which you interact with the people around you. It can lead to you attempting to change the way you live to accommodate those feelings of anxiety, especially if you consider the states of anxiety that involve phobias or other fears that may become debilitating.

If left untreated, this can destroy lives. It can leave you feeling unable to get out. It can ruin relationships if you continue to put off meeting up or constantly change the way that you want to interact with people. You need to be able to better deal with the people in your life and to better deal with your anxiety if you hope to enjoy a happy life.

When it comes down to it, upwards of 4o million people in the

US alone suffer from anxiety disorders. It is the most frequently diagnosed mental health issue in the entire country. However, you can learn to defeat this; you can learn how to overcome these feelings of anxiety, and the best way to do so is through the use of the vagus nerve.

ANTI-ANXIETY STRATEGIES

Anti-anxiety strategies are a skill that you learn; just as with physical exercise, practice is required.

With a little effort, you can train your mind to feel safe. Safety signals prevent your fear and anxiety reactions from being triggered. Choose an anxiety prevention strategy, and try it until you feel less anxious. If one doesn't work for you, try another. The goal is to find exercises that can quickly help you relax.

1. Stay Present Through Mindfulness

Mindfulness is the practice of being present and without judgement in your current state and environment.

To get out of your thoughts and into the present:

- Find a quiet, comfortable place to sit and close your eyes.
- Notice how your breathing and body feel.
- Now move your awareness to the sensations that you observe in your environment. Ask what's going on outside of your body? Notice what you listen to, smell and sense in your environment.
- Change your consciousness from your body to your surroundings and vice versa several times, until your anxiety subsides.

2.Interrupt your Fearful Thinking

It can be challenging to think clearly when you feel anxious.

Sometimes an anxious thought can lead us to believe in harmful thoughts that are wrong, or to do things that make our fear worse. It can be helpful to break up or interrupt your anxious thoughts so that you can think clearly and respond appropriately to your thoughts.

Try different methods to interrupt your anxious thinking process:

- Sing a silly song about your fears optimistically, or speak about your fears in a funny voice.
- Choose a nice thought that you can focus on instead of worrying. It could be someone you love, your happy place, or something you look forward to later in the day, such as a good dinner.
- Listen to music or read a book
- Be aware of when you shift your focus from fear to a task and write down how you feel.

3. Think about How Fear Affects your Life.

"Three of the most common characteristics of a person with an anxiety disorder are perfectionism, which requires the consent of others and the need for control," said John Tsilimparis, MFT, director of Anxiety and Panic Disorder Center in Los Angeles and one of the therapists at A& E's Obsessed; a program for severe anxiety disorders.

4. Set Up a Structure.

Time-out often leads to rethinking and over-reinforcement, said Tsilimparis. In other words, if you are not excited or busy, you are likely to focus on trivial things and be obsessed with them. He therefore helps his clients develop daily newspapers to plan their days and to include healthy activities.

5. Fight Twisted Thoughts.

Your own thoughts can stir up fear. For example, asking 'What if?' or judging yourself only as a success or a failure in the things you do.

"You can't be afraid if you don't let unsafe thinking rule your life," said Joseph Luciani, PhD, clinical psychologist and author of "Self-Coaching: The Powerful Program Against Anxiety and Depression."

"Think of your thoughts as a wheel," said Luciani. "When you spin this wheel, you create sparks - sparks of fear, 'What if I fail?'"What if I get sick? If you stop turning the wheel, the thoughts of insecurity stop."

Identify these distorted thoughts and think about the stress they cause, Tsilimparis said. Then try to substitute the thoughts with something more balanced. Keep practicing. Over time, balanced thoughts become automatic.

6. Give Up Control.

According to Luciani, many of us try to control life in order to feel less vulnerable and insecure. We aren't sure if we are able to "manage life moment by moment," he said. Trying to control life is not a certainty, and preparing for a potential hazard creates both psychological and physiological stress that only exhausts and leads to anxiety. So the key is to recognize and accept that you cannot control life.

7. Check your Reactions.

"Although we cannot control the world, we can control our response to it," said Tsilimparis. "It gives you the opportunity to realize that you don't have to be a victim of life, the world, and Highway 405 (in California)." Realize that you are responsible for your luck and your life. You can change.

8. Trust Yourself.

"Confidence is the ability to believe that you can do what life has in store for you," said Luciani. Trusting yourself means reducing uncertainty - which Luciani sees as a habit we can change. According to Luciani, self-confidence is a muscle: "When you are afraid, your self-confidence muscle is atrophied, and your insecurity is related to muscles."

Strengthen your muscles by taking small risks.

If you are concerned, there might be a small risk of saying, "I will take the risk of believing that I can do a good job," said Luciani. He gave another example in which perfectionists accepted that they were good enough. If you practice this acceptance, your confidence will increase and you will see that life can be managed more spontaneously.

9. Practice Yoga.

Anxiety usually includes raging thoughts, recurring worries, and an animated body. According to Mary Nurrie-Stearns, certified clinical social worker, yoga teacher, and co-author of 'Yoga for Anxiety: Meditations and methods to calm your mind and body', yoga can help manage all of these symptoms by calming both your mind and your body. Just concentrating on breathing, conveying and pronouncing a mantra has a calming effect. One yoga practice is no better than another.

Studies show that fear matters, Nurrie-Stearns said. Research has shown that gentle, restful, and soothing poses are best when there is serious trauma. When the body is tense, strong poses or poses that last longer can penetrate deep areas of body tension. When there are tremors and an increase in heart rate, a flow yoga exercise helps to relieve accelerated anxiety. Start your workout by following the lessons of a professional yoga teacher.

You can also practice yoga at home. Nurrie-Stearns suggested the following routine:

- Sit on your yoga mat daily with your favorite drink
- Take a few minutes to concentrate on breathing
- Read a line with something inspiring, be it a sentence from a poem, a sacred text, or a mantra and commit to doing at least one yoga pose

10. "Wink" at your Thoughts.

Nurrie-Stearns' techniques are specific to yoga, but you can use this technique at any time. Experiencing our thoughts helps us not to be caught by them. "When you wink at a thought, you notice the mental chatter, say 'I see you' and draw your attention back to your breath. In other words, we recognize the thought, we allow it and let it go." As Nurrie-Stearns emphasizes, our minds are constantly generating thoughts. So why not repeat those thoughts which "feed and soothe" us?

11. Distinguish Fact from Fiction.

Worry is a fiction. It is "an anticipation of future problems. Because your future exists only as a mental construct, worrying about a future event is fiction," said Luciani. He gave a fictitious example: "I have high blood pressure, I will have a heart attack." And a worrying fact: "I have high blood pressure and if I want to avoid a heart attack, I have to change my eating habits and do sports." The concern is based on facts and is addressed today.

12. Stop Relying on the Consent of People.

As Tsilimparis said, relying on the consent of others can also lead to fear. To stop this from happening over time, pay attention to how you interact with others and when you want. For example, when do you say yes to someone when you really want to say no?

Raise your awareness and slowly start changing your behavior. Before participating in an activity, please consider how you will react and do what is right for you. Another therapist once said to Tsilimparis: "Here's the problem with people's joy: there is good news and bad news. The good news is that people really don't care; and the bad news is that people really don't care. "

9. Relax While Breathing

If you feel anxious, you may notice that your heart rate and breathing become a little faster. You will also notice a little sweating and may start to feel dizzy. When you are anxious, controlling your breathing can relax your mind and body.

To control your breathing when you are anxious, do the following:
- Sit in a quiet, comfortable place.
- Place one of your hands on your chest and the other on your stomach. Your stomach should move around more than your chest when you take a deep breath.
- Breathe in slowly and regularly through your nose. Watch and feel your hands as you breathe. The hand on your chest should stay calm while the hand on your stomach moves slightly.
- Exhale slowly through your mouth.
- Repeat this process at least 10 times or until you are less anxious.

10. Relax While Watching

Find your happy place. By imagining a place where you feel relaxed, you can actually calm your brain and body. When you start feeling anxious, sit in a quiet, comfortable place. Think of your perfect place to relax. It can be anywhere in the world, real or imaginary, but it must be an image that you find very comforting, happy, peaceful, and safe. Make it easy for you to think about it so that you can refer to it in the future if you feel anxious.

Think of all the little details you would find if you were there. Think about how the place feels, looks and sounds. Imagine yourself in this place and enjoy it comfortably.

When you have a good picture of your "happy place", close your eyes and breathe slowly and regularly through your nose and mouth. Pay attention to your breathing and continue to focus on the place you imagined in your head, until you feel your anxiety decrease. Visit this place in your head if you feel anxious.

11. Relax your muscles

If you feel anxious, you may notice tension in your muscles. This muscle strain can make your anxiety more difficult to manage the moment you experience it. By relieving your muscles of stress, you can usually reduce your anxiety.

How to quickly relieve your muscle tension in moments of fear:

- Sit in a quiet, comfortable place. Close your eyes, be calm and focus on your breathing. Breathe slowly through your nose and mouth.
- Use your hand to clench your fist tightly.
- Hold your fist for a few seconds. Notice the tension you feel in your hand.
- Slowly open your fingers and pay attention to how you feel. You may notice a feeling of tension leave your hand. Ultimately, your hand becomes lighter and more relaxed.
- Continue stretching and then release various muscle groups from your body, hands, legs, shoulders or feet. You may want to move your body up and down by stretching different muscle groups. Avoid straining the muscles in an area of your body where you are injured or in pain, as this could make your injury worse.

12. Relax by Counting

Counting is an easy way to relieve your anxiety. If you feel anxious, find a quiet, comfortable place to sit. Close your eyes and count focusedly to 10. Repeat the process and count to 20 or higher. Keep counting until you feel your fear decrease.

Sometimes this relief happens quickly, but sometimes it can take a while. Keep calm and patient. Counting can help you unwind because it gives you something to focus on in addition to your fear. It's a great method to use in a congested or busy space, such as a store or train, where other anxiety exercises may be more difficult.

Anxiety exercises may not work for everybody and may worsen symptoms in people diagnosed with Generalized Anxiety Disorder (GAD). There are many apps which can offer a variety of techniques, from natural sounds to acupressure. However, if your fear often affects your daily life, happiness, and activities, you should ask a mental health professional for help.

BRAIN PLASTICITY

The old theory that DNA cannot be changed and that you cling to what you were born with is now being refuted. Researchers have found that your DNA actually changes based on your experience, your emotions, and your environment.

Our views of the brain have changed, as have our views of DNA. Science has affirmed more evidence that your brain is flexible and continually adapts to your lifestyle, your physiology, and your environment. This notion is termed neuroplasticity, or brain plasticity, which means that you literally reform your brain with each passing day. Your brain has the extraordinary ability to reconstruct paths, make new connections and neurons (nerve cells) throughout your life.

For example, your brain can shift functions from a damaged area to an undamaged area. It also is able to change its physical structure. When a new skill is acquired, the more you focus and practice it, the better you get. It is the result of new neural pathways that form in response to your learning efforts. In the meantime, your brain is also "synaptically circumcised", i.e. pathways that you no longer use are eliminated. This phenomenon even applies to emotional states. For example, if you have been scared in the past, your nerve tracts will be wired for fear. However, if you acquire means to feel calm, relaxed, and peaceful, these fear paths are cut off from lack of activity.

As a result, you may realise that your brain's plasticity is highly dependent on your lifestyle. The foods you eat, the amount of physical activity, your emotional states, and your sleep patterns all affect how your brain works. Therefore, you can do a lot to maintain, or even increase, your brain power.

CHRONIC STRESS AND THE VAGUS NERVE

If you are in stressful situations, you activate your sympathetic nervous system. In an ideal situation the stress will dissipate, and your body activates the parasympathetic nervous system to relax again. But sometimes this does not happen at all or within a healthy time frame. This means your body continues to respond in a heightened, stressful state, and problems start to manifest.

From a neurological standpoint, two things begin to happen:

1. Activation of the brain-intestine axis

2. Activation of the hypothalamus-pituitary-adrenal axis

Your brain feels stressed and anxious for a long time, so it creates more hormones, or CRF's. These start in the hypothalamus and then travel to your pituitary gland. Here they create another hormone to release into your body, ACTH. This moves from the pituitary to the bloodstream and finally off to the adrenal glands. Once there, the influx of hormones triggers adrenaline and cortisol production. This creation is what suppresses your immune system function and precursors to inflammation. This explains why when you are suffering from anxiety and chronic stress, you can get sick more easily.

This can ultimately end in depression because it is a disorder many have linked to the brain's response of inflammation.

But there is more that happens when the body is suffering from anxiety and chronic stress. Your body also increases glutamate in your brain. This is another neurotransmitter that can cause symptoms such as migraines, more anxiety, and depression, especially at excessive levels. Increased levels of cortisol also shrink the physical volume of your hippocampus. This is the section of your brain responsible for forming new memories.

HOW TO HANDLE STRESS

The best way to treat this situation is to prevent your body from remaining in this state and learn how to stimulate your vagus nerve and allow your body to "override" the sympathetic response. You need to care for your vagus nerve and keep it acting properly so you can "slam on the brakes" of fight, flight, or freeze, and let yourself relax.

Remember, your vagal tone is a biological process that identifies the vagus nerve's activity levels. Increasing your vagal tone means increasing your relaxation. Your Parasympathetic system is activated, and you can "handle" stress a lot easier. This positively impacts the balance of your emotions and general well-being.

Breathe more slowly and you will feel calmer. Not necessarily happy, but stable. Slow breathing is boring, but it's very effective.

"When you are in a stressful situation," said Norcliffe-Kaufmann, "and you say to yourself: how should I react, how should I react? - If you consciously slow down your breathing for just a minute or a few seconds, you can put yourself in a calmer state so that you can communicate better. "

"Your body recognizes your breathing and adjusts your heart rate in response," Norcliffe-Kaufmann states. "When we breathe," she explains, "the sensory nodes in our lungs ("pulmonary stretch receptors") send information through the vagus nerve into the brain, and when we exhale, the brain sends information through to the vagus nerve to slow the heart down or to accelerate. When we breathe slowly, the heart slows down and we relax. Conversely, when we breathe quickly, our heart speeds up and we feel intensified or fearful."

It is specifically the exhalation that triggers the relaxation response; Norcliffe-Kaufmann confirmed: "Vagal activity is highest and heart rate is lowest when you exhale", mentioning that the ideal and most soothing way to do a breathing exercise is six times a minute: five seconds in, five seconds out. She also noted that in the study which determined this rate, the researchers found that this type of slow breathing is also what practitioners do during meditation with mantras and or while saying the Hail Mary with a rosary. "Whenever you say the rosary or a meditation mantra," said Norcliffe-Kaufmann, "it naturally synchronizes your breathing six times a minute."

Take a deep breath. Hug a friend. Stretch your limbs. Each of these simple actions gives a feeling of calm and comfort.

Some other practices that are believed to improve vagal tone (beyond deep, slow breathing) include laughing, singing, buzzing, yoga, acupuncture, and splashing cold water on your face - or a full cold rinse.

TRAUMA, PTSD AND VAGUS NERVE

Post-traumatic stress disorder (PTSD) is a condition that can develop in people who have suffered or witnessed a traumatic, catastrophic or violent event, or who have become aware of a traumatic experience that has happened to a loved one. We all may have overwhelming, frightening and perceived experiences that are beyond our control, such as being involved in a car accident or being assaulted. In particular, some professional figures - for example, military personnel, members of law enforcement, medical personnel or firefighters - are more likely to be exposed to particularly violent and shocking incidents or details.

Most people manage to overcome the initial shock without the need for additional support, but if the victim's suffering is prolonged for more than a month after exposure to the trauma and significantly interferes with the individual's work, social or school life, a diagnosis of PTSD should be made.

To make a diagnosis of PTSD it is necessary to assess the presence of the following criteria:

Criterion A - Exposure to A Traumatic Event
- Exposure to traumatic event such as war, torture, death threats;
- car crashes, robbery, plane crashes;
- illnesses with an unfortunate prognosis;
- complicated or traumatic grief;
- mistreatment
- physical and sexual abuse
- bullying;
- assault, death threats, serious injury.

Criterion B - Symptoms of Reliving traumatic events
The victim repeatedly relives the moment of trauma. For

example, this can take the form of flashbacks, i.e. the perception of being re-experiencing the event in the present, until the complete loss of awareness of the surrounding environment. Flashbacks are usually accompanied by intense fear and physiological reactivity (rapid heartbeat, sweating, muscle tension and nausea).

Criterion C - Avoidance Symptoms

In an attempt to avoid re-experiencing the trauma, the victim may begin to avoid external situations (activities, conversations, people, etc.) that remind, symbolize or are somehow associated with the traumatic event. Over time, this coping strategy becomes more and more problematic as the person may end up withdrawing from social interactions, stopping going to habitual places, or significantly changing their habits so as not to run into details that may trigger disturbing symptoms.

Criterion D - Symptoms of Negative Alteration of Thoughts and Emotions

Negative emotions commonly experienced by victims include guilt, shame, anger, fear and feelings of depression. To protect themselves from psychological pain, the person may try to detach themselves from their emotions, and may be insensitive, disinterested or alienated from others, even when they are loved ones or activities that previously brought them joy.

Criterion E - Symptoms of Hyperactivation

Human beings are evolutionarily programmed to fight or escape from situations that are dangerous at a given moment, but when the danger ceases the same thing typically happens for the state of activation that made the defensive response of flight or fight of the sympathetic system possible. However, in the case of PTSD, this defensive mode is constantly activated. The person develops a sort of hypersensitivity to potential danger signals, which leads him/her to be constantly on alert, to respond in an explosive and angry manner even in the absence of provocation and to live in a state of hypervigilance and tension that interferes with the ability to calm down or fall asleep.

PTSD is therefore a condition in which the vagus nerve has never had a chance to fully activate. Normally, after something stressful has happened, a relaxation process is triggered,, governed by the parasympathetic system, which inhibits prolonged "flight or fight" reactions of the sympathetic system, restoring the homeostatic balance of our body, fundamental for good health.

However, when PTSD occurs, it is believed the body never turned on that parasympathetic state the the vagus nerve is responsible for encouraging. Without the relax response, the body continues to suffer as if it were still stuck in the traumatic experience. Memory becomes distorted and disrupted, Emotions remain volatile.

However, this means that, with the proper sort of engagement, you can start to pull yourself out of that sort of state. To help relieve the anxiety that occurs with PTSD, you need to be able to stimulate the vagus nerve to activate it again. It is only by getting back to that parasympathetic normalcy that you can begin to live again.

DEPRESSION AND THE VAGUS NERVE

DEFINING DEPRESSION

Depression is a severe mental disorder that can affect how you feel act and think.

Depression is much more than just feeling low or being in a bad mood. It is a mental state that is characterized by emotional detachment, feelings of sadness or loss, and a lack of interest in activities. Depression is a serious mental illness that has been linked to suicide and destructive social behavior.

Is it possible to determine the cause of depression? While it is not possible to single out a single factor as the main course of depression, social factors, biological, and psychological sources of distress have been found to be predisposing factors that lead to depressive tendencies.

This distress that is initiated by a combination of these factors alters and impairs brain function resulting in psychological and even physical disorders.

Depression weakens your immune system, leaving you susceptible to infections that your body could easily ward off if you were not depressed.

It has also been associated with poor weight management. Have you ever noticed that you tend to either eat too much when you are feeling low or to not eat at all? Depression has an undeniable effect on our weight. While binge eating after you have had a stressful day will probably not have long term effects on your health, people with chronic depression develop long-term bad eating habits, which ultimately impact their health.

Indecision and lack of clarity of thought are common in people with depression and can be aggravated by other effects of depression such as fatigue and insomnia, which also affect our alertness and ability to focus.

Beyond the physical and mental disorders, depression impacts our capacity to engage with others. Depressed people will more often than not withdraw from friends and relatives, become emotionally detached, and lose interest in physical contact, including sexual activity.

Decreased neuronal plasticity and chronic inflammation of the brain may result from chronic depression. Stimulation of the vagus nerve has been shown to inhibit inflammation and help in combating social distress by alleviating anxiety and fear; this improves our ability to engage socially with others, and in effect, helps in combating the emotional detachment that is associated with depression. The effects of the vagus nerve responses on stress management are also key factors in helping people recover faster from depression, thereby helping prevent the mental effects of prolonged depressive states. In 2005, the FDA endorsed the use of vagus nerve stimulation to treat treatment-resistant depression (TRD)

HOW TO FIGHT DEPRESSION

Depression can drain your energy, and this can hinder your desire to seek treatment.

However, there are small steps that can be taken to help you improve your overall sense of well-being.

1. Be Open

Depression is widespread. It affects millions of people, including some you may know. Every day of life with this disorder is different.

The key to self-treatment for depression is being open,

accepting and loving yourself and what you are going through.

2. If You Have to Wallow, Do It - But Do It Constructively

Suppressing your feelings and emotions seems to be a strategic way to deal with the negative symptoms of depression. But this technique is ultimately unhealthy. If you have a bad day, own it. Let the emotions feel - but don't stay there. Think about what you're going through, by writing or recording. Experiencing the ebb and flow of depressive symptoms can be revealing for self-healing and hope.

3. Know That Today Does Not Indicate Tomorrow

Today's mood, feelings or thoughts do not belong to tomorrow. If you haven't gotten up today or achieved your goals, remember that you haven't missed the opportunity to try again tomorrow.

5. Do The Opposite of What The "Voice of Depression" Suggests

The negative and irrational voice in your head can talk you out of self-help. However, if you can teach yourself to recognize it, you can learn to replace it. Use logic as a weapon. Address each thought individually as it arises.

6. Set Achievable Goals

A long list of tasks can be so extensive that you'd rather not do anything. Instead of putting together a long list of tasks, you should define one or two smaller goals.

For example:

Don't clean the house. Take out the trash.

Do not do all of the laundry that is piled up. Simply sort the batteries by color.

Do not empty your entire inbox. Just send urgent messages.

If you've done one thing, keep your eyes on another thing, then another. This way you get a list of concrete successes and not a list of tasks to be done.

7. Reward Your Efforts

All goals deserve to be recognized and all achievements deserve to be celebrated. When you reach a goal, do your best to recognize it. You may not want to celebrate with cakes and confetti but recognizing your own success can be a very powerful weapon against the negative weight of depression.

8. Creating A Routine Can Help

If symptoms of depression disrupt your daily routine, a schedule will help you stay in control. However, these plans do not have to be planned for THE whole day.

Concentrate on the times when you feel worst organized or absent-minded.

Your schedule can focus on the hour before work or just before bed. It may be reserved for weekends. Concentrate on creating a casual but structured routine that will help you keep up your daily rhythm.

9. Do Something You Love ...

Depression can cause you to give in to your tiredness. It may seem more powerful than happy feelings. Try to grow again and do something that you enjoy - something that is relaxing but still stimulating. It may be playing an instrument, painting, walking or cycling. These activities can subtly improve your mood and energy and help you overcome your symptoms.

10.Listen to Music

Music is a great way to improve your mood and relieve symptoms of depression. It can also help you strengthen your source of positive emotions.

11. Spend Time in Nature

Mother nature can have a strong impact on depression. The

Research Source Trust suggests that people who spend time in the wild see improvements to their mental health. Sun exposure can offer some of the same benefits. It can increase your serotonin level, which can be a temporary source of trust. Consider walking among the trees for lunch or spending time in a park. Or plan a weekend hike. These projects can help you reconnect with nature while absorbing a few rays.

12. Spend Time with Loved Ones

Depression can make you isolate yourself and withdraw from friends and family. Face to face time, however, can help eliminate these tendencies. If you can't spend time in person, phone calls or video chats can also be helpful. Try to remember that these people CAN take care of you. Resist the temptation to feel like a burden. You need interaction.

13. Try Something Completely New

When you do the same thing every day, you use the same parts of your brain. You can challenge your neurons and change the chemistry of your brain by doing something completely different.

Research also shows that doing new things can improve your general well-being and strengthen your social relationships. To take advantage of these benefits, you should try a new sport, take a creative course, or learn a new baking technique.

14. Volunteering

Spend time with other people and do something new - by volunteering and devoting your time to someone or something else, can help you improve your mental health even more.

15. Practice Gratitude

If you do something that you enjoy, or if you discover a new activity that you enjoy, you may be able to further improve your mental health by taking the time to be grateful.

Research has shown that gratitude can have lasting positive

effects on your overall mental health.

In addition, writing your gratitude - including writing notes to others - can be particularly important.

16. The Integration of Meditation Can Help Anchor Your Thoughts

Research has revealed that activities such as meditation, yoga and deep breathing can help you improve your well-being and feel more connected to what's going on around you.

17. What You Feed On Can Also Affect Your Well-Being

There is no magic diet that treats depression. But what you put in your body can have a real and significant impact on how you feel. A diet full of lean meats, vegetables, and grains can be a good place to start. Try to avoid stimulants like caffeine, coffee and sodas, and depressants like alcohol.

Some people also feel strengthened and have more energy if they avoid sugar, preservatives and processed foods. If you can afford it, you should seek advice from a doctor or nutritionist.

18. When You Are Ready to Practice, Consider Walking Around the Block

On days when you feel like you cannot get up, exercise seems to be the last thing you want to do. However, exercise and physical activity can be strong fighters for depression.

Research suggests that exercise can be just as effective for some people as medication to relieve depression symptoms. It can also help prevent future depressive episodes.

If you can, go around the block. Start with a five-minute walk and climb up from there.

19. Sufficient Sleep Can Also Make Itself Felt

Sleep disorders are common with depression. You don't sleep well, or you sleep too much. Both can worsen the symptoms of depression.

Plan for eight hours of sleep a night. Try to achieve a sound sleep.

Going to bed and getting out of bed at a regular time each day can help you with your daily routine. If you sleep properly, you can also feel more balanced and energetic throughout the day.

20. Consider Clinical Treatment

It can also be of help to talk to a professional about what you're going through. An expert can refer you to a therapist or other specialist.

They can assess your symptoms and help you develop a clinical treatment plan tailored to your needs. This can include traditional options like medication and therapy or alternative measures like acupuncture.

YOUR BABY'S VAGUS NERVE

BABY MASSAGE

Several researchers have wondered, over time, whether it is better for infants to be massaged with firm or gentle pressure.

In fact, most studies show that good pressure is much more effective in terms of health and well-being than mild pressure. We are always talking about quantities that cannot be measured exactly, but let's say that in comparison there are:

- a "moderate pressure", which embraces the tissues and perceives the body tone, without touching the bones...
- and a "light pressure", a very gentle pressure, like a caress.

Two researches in particular, conducted with children born before the term, have evaluated the wellbeing deriving from the execution of massages with the two different pressures. In both studies, infants were massaged several times a day for 5 days and the researchers measured behavioral status, stress levels, heart rate, vagal activity and gastric motility before and after each session, as well as monitoring weight purchase. Children massaged with moderate pressure, compared to those massaged with mild pressure, were found to have experienced the following results:

- strong increase in vagal tone
- significant weight gain in the babies every single day
- Significant decrease in agitation during sleep and wakefulness
- significant decrease in crying
- significant decrease in movement
- significant reduction in stress-related behaviour (e.g. hiccups)

- substantial slowing of the heartbeat

Therefore, we can say that the massage performed with moderate pressure, increasing the vagal tone, helps children to react better to stress, decreases their agitation and makes the whole digestive system work better.

In conclusion: no matter how small your babies are and what difficulties they have, don't be afraid to touch and massage them: stay, with your hands still or moving rhythmically, close to them, giving your energy and caring for their body and soul.

VAGUS NERVE AND EMOTIONAL MATURATION OF THE CHILD

One of the essential skills in the emotional sphere is knowing how to calm yourself when you're upset.

This ability is learned in early childhood and perfected in later years. The first source of learning is the caregiver, usually the mother, who, when she hears the baby crying, takes him in her arms and cradles him with love until he calms down. This instinctive gesture, according to some theories, is a real biological attunement through which the baby learns how to obtain the same result on its own.

Between 10 and 18 months of age the child experiences a critical period in which the orbifrontal area of the prefrontal cortex quickly forms connections with the limbic system (our emotional system) becoming a fundamental switch to trigger or defuse suffering. From this moment on, the child who experiences endless episodes of consolation from others is helped to learn how to calm down by strengthening the connections of this circuit, and the more consolation he receives the more skilled he will become in the art of self-consolation.

Another circuit is involved in the emotional maturation of the child: the vagus nerve.

The vagus nerve not only regulates cardiac and visceral function, but also transmits signals from the adrenal glands to the amygdala (a crucial structure of our emotional system, the limbic system), preparing it to secrete the catecholamines that trigger the reaction and escape response.

A study conducted at Washington University a few years ago showed that the very fact of having emotionally capable parents favored an improvement in the vagal function of the child.

What does it mean to be emotionally capable parents?

It means guiding one's children in their emotional lives by talking to them about their feelings and explaining how to understand them, avoiding criticism and making judgments, calmly resolving problems posed by difficult emotional situations (e.g. separations), showing them alternatives to despair, physical confrontation or arrogance, and teaching them to tolerate frustration.

When parents perform this task well, children behave better, as they can effectively suppress the vagal activity that induces the amygdala to prepare the body for combat or escape.

What parents call "whim" is actually a "language", a language that describes the level of attunement between the child and the parent, the degree of empathy of the parent towards the child in the recognition and satisfaction of his emotional needs.

Often, unfortunately, the selfishness of adults, dependent on the impulse to compulsively satisfy their needs, transforms the emotional needs of the child into an obstacle that steals time, space and energy from themselves, in the face of which the quickest and most emotionally economical solution is to ignore the child, punish him, raise your voice.

Let's remember then that each of us has a tool to regulate the vagal activity of our children (and basically also of ourselves) as powerful as a dose of tranquilizers: love, care and patience.

CONCLUSION

Thank you for making it through to the end of *the Vagus Nerve*. We hope it was informative and able to provide you with all of the tools you need to tap into the power of the vagus nerve and stimulate your body's self-healing mechanism.

The next step is to start applying the techniques that you have learned in this book.

It is time to decide what exercises you want to try and put them into action. It is not enough to just read about all the functions of the vagus nerve and how it can be stimulated or balanced. It is now time to apply your knowledge and change your life.

The vagus nerve plays an important part in our overall health and wellbeing and getting the best possible vagal tone will lead to numerous benefits for your health.